USBORNE
ILLUSTRATED
ADVENTURE
STORIES

CONTENTS

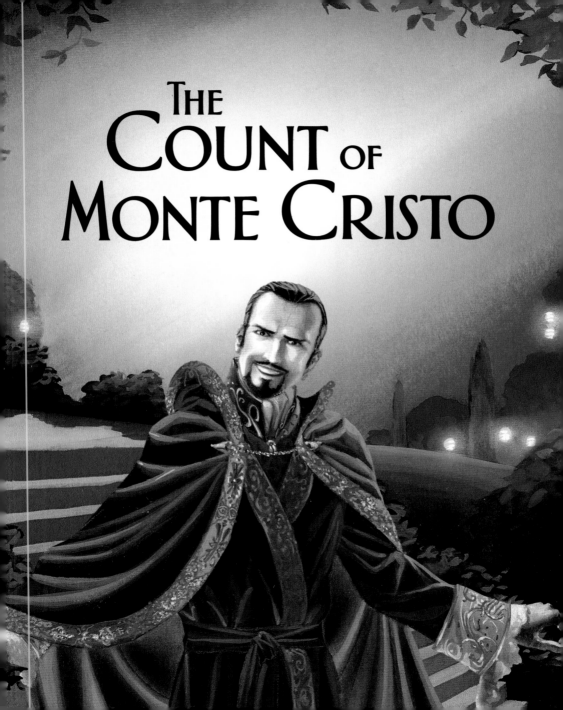

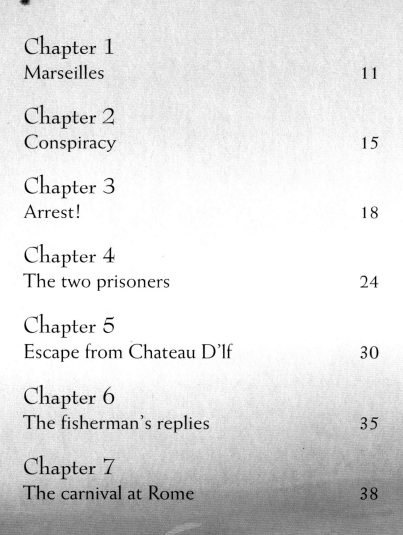

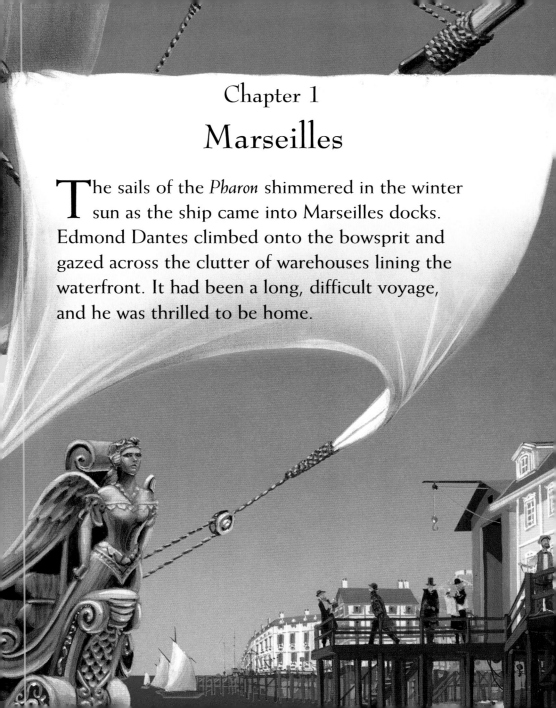

Chapter 1
Marseilles

The sails of the *Pharon* shimmered in the winter sun as the ship came into Marseilles docks. Edmond Dantes climbed onto the bowsprit and gazed across the clutter of warehouses lining the waterfront. It had been a long, difficult voyage, and he was thrilled to be home.

But on the docks, Mr. Morrel, the ship's owner, greeted him with a worried frown. "Where is Captain Leclere?" he asked.

Edmond smiled sadly. He told Mr. Morrel how Captain Leclere had died of fever. As second mate, he had taken command of the ship himself for the rest of their trade voyage.

"But there is something Dantes has not reported," a voice said. It was Danglars, the ship's accountant. He was a shrewd-looking man who always had a sneer on his face, especially for Edmond.

"Edmond has not said that we stopped at Elba," he told Mr. Morrel.

Morrel's face darkened. The island of Elba was where France's previous ruler, Napoleon Bonaparte, was being held prisoner. All ships were banned from stopping there.

"Is this true?" Mr. Morrel asked.

"It is," Edmond said. "Before Captain Leclere died, he asked me to deliver a letter to the island."

"Then it is settled," Morrel announced. "Edmond was simply loyal to his captain. As I am sure others will be to him."

"You mean *Edmond* is to be made captain?" Danglars seethed.

"I do," Morrel said. "If you accept Edmond?"

A beaming smile spread across Edmond's face. But before he could reply, he saw a beautiful woman running towards him.

It was Mercedes, his fiancée. She leaped into Edmond's arms, blushing with delight. As they kissed, though, Edmond spotted a gloomy figure watching them from the shadows.

"Who are you sir?" he demanded.

Mercedes pulled the man closer. "Edmond, this is my cousin Fernand. He looked after me while you were away."

Edmond grasped Fernand's hand and shook it firmly. "Then you can be the first to hear, Fernand. I am to become captain of the *Pharon*, and tomorrow Mercedes will become my wife!"

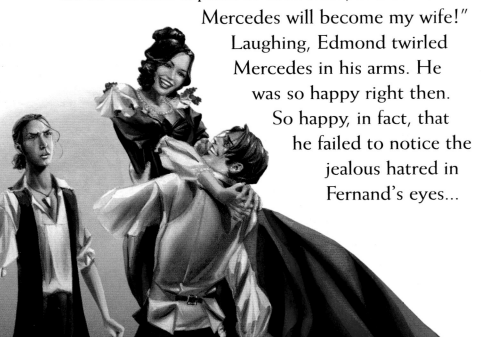

Laughing, Edmond twirled Mercedes in his arms. He was so happy right then. So happy, in fact, that he failed to notice the jealous hatred in Fernand's eyes...

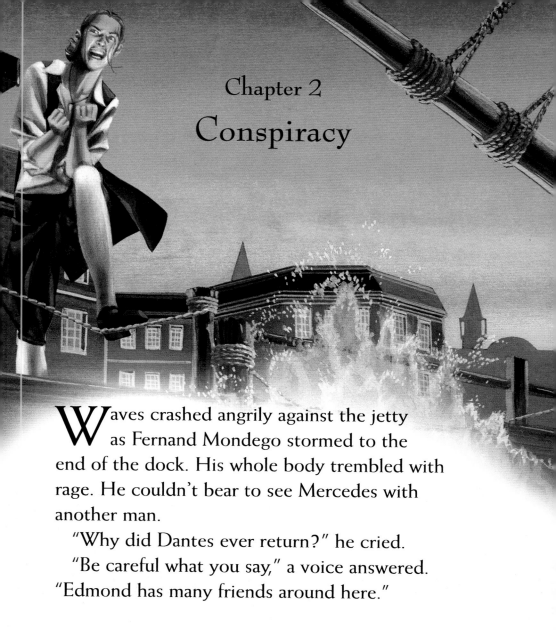

Chapter 2
Conspiracy

Waves crashed angrily against the jetty as Fernand Mondego stormed to the end of the dock. His whole body trembled with rage. He couldn't bear to see Mercedes with another man.

"Why did Dantes ever return?" he cried.

"Be careful what you say," a voice answered. "Edmond has many friends around here."

Danglars sat outside a tavern, with his accounts papers spread across a table.

"What do you want?" Fernand spat.

"Merely to share a toast," Danglars said, pouring a glass of wine. "To Edmond Dantes, future captain of the *Pharon* and husband to the fair Mercedes."

Fernand's face turned livid red. He snatched Danglars' glass and smashed it to the floor. "I hate Edmond Dantes!" he cried.

Calmly, Danglars poured himself another drink. He too hated Dantes. He had worked hard on the

Pharon, and felt that it should be him, not Edmond, who was made captain. "What if there was a way to make him go away again?" he said. "You could marry Mercedes and I would become captain."

"If only there was," Fernand groaned, "then I would do it, however hard."

Danglars' lips curled into a sinister smile. He rustled among his papers, finding a blank sheet. Then he dipped his quill into his inkpot. "It is not hard at all," he said. "We simply have to write a letter."

Chapter 3
Arrest!

The following night, at the same tavern where
Fernand and Danglars wrote their letter, excited
guests gathered for a wedding feast. Edmond wore
his best suit and his biggest smile, while Mercedes'
eyes sparkled with joy. Everyone agreed they had
never seen such a happy couple.

The tavern rang so loudly with laughter that no one
heard the miserable moan from the back of the room.

Fernand sat with his head hung in despair. "I cannot bear to watch," he told Danglars. "You said that our letter would solve everything. But still Mercedes is about to be married."

"Have faith," Danglars said. "I think I hear our plan working now..."

Just then, five soldiers marched into the tavern, armed with rifles. Their captain stormed up to Edmond. "Edmond Dantes?" he said. "I arrest you in the name of the law."

Mercedes reached to hold Edmond back, but he simply smiled and stepped forward.

"You must be mistaken," he said. "I have never committed a crime in my life."

The captain waggled a sheet of paper in Edmond's face. "This letter says otherwise."

Dear sir, it is my duty to inform you that Edmond Dantes, mate of the ship Pharon, recently docked at the island of Elba carrying a letter for the traitor Napoleon Bonaparte...

"Who wrote this?" Edmond asked.

"Do you deny that it is true?"

"I do not, but—"

"Then you must come with us."

Before Edmond could reply, the soldiers grabbed his arm and yanked him away. As they dragged him from the room, he saw the startled faces on all of his guests — except for two. Fernand and Danglars were smiling.

Dark clouds gathered over the docks as the soldiers marched Edmond from the tavern. One thrust him into a boat. The others climbed in beside him and began rowing from the dock.

"Please," Edmond begged, "where are you taking me?"

"See for yourself," one of the men grunted.

And then Edmond did. They were headed for a craggy island beyond the bay, from which a stone fortress rose to the soot-black sky. That fortress was Chateau D'If, a grim prison for traitors.

Suddenly, Edmond flung himself across the boat.
But before he could escape over the side, one of the
guards clubbed him on the head with his rifle.

Edmond slumped to the watery deck. He lay
groaning, too dazed to fight, as the boat bashed
against another dock. The guards lifted him from the
deck and up some stone steps.

Lightning blazed across the sky. Chateau D'If
loomed over Edmond in ghastly silhouette. Thunder
roared around the old prison's crumbling walls.

Edmond was hurled into a dingy cell.

A guard leaned over him, his face ghostly white in the glare of his lantern. "Welcome to your new home," he said.

The door slammed shut. Edmond was left alone in the dark.

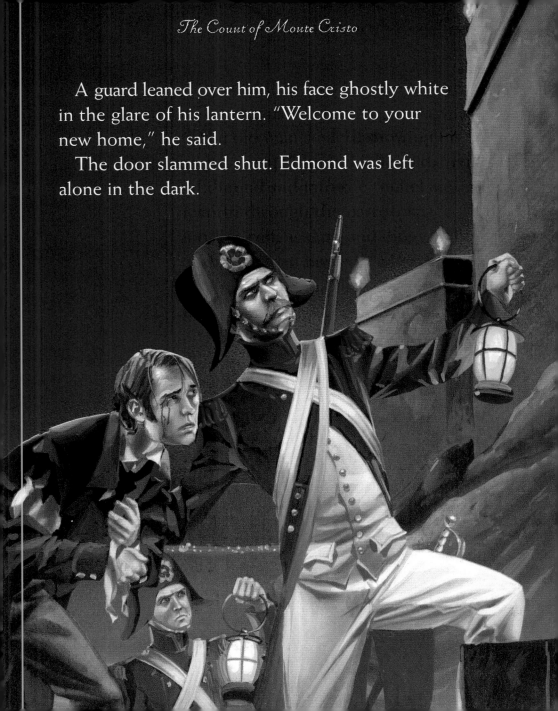

Chapter 4
The two prisoners

For hours, Edmond sat slumped against the cell wall, clutching his knees to his chest. He was convinced he would be released any moment. But that moment never came.

Hours turned into days. Slowly, Edmond's confusion boiled into anger.

"I am innocent!" he yelled.

Days became weeks and then months. Edmond curled up in the dark, haunted by memories. At first he thought about Mercedes, but more and more he became obsessed with Fernand and Danglars. He was certain they wrote the letter accusing him of treason.

Months grew into years. By then, Edmond's wedding suit hung like rags around his skeleton frame. His nails grew long and filthy, and lice crawled in his tangled beard.

All day, the scurrying sound of rats echoed around his cramped cell. The noise seemed to be coming from under the ground. Edmond pressed his ear to the floor, listening for hours. How he envied their freedom!

Then, one day, the ground began to tremble. One of the stones shuddered and rose.

Edmond scrabbled back in fright as a head emerged from the ground – a tangled mass of white hair and beard with two bulging eyes in between. It was another prisoner!

The old man glared at Edmond cowering in the corner. "Curses!" he cried. "I have dug the wrong way. I thought I was escaping the prison, not digging deeper inside."

Edmond crawled closer and peered into the man's tunnel. For the first time in years, a smile spread across his filthy face. "Let me help you dig in the other direction," he said.

"It would take years," the man replied.

"I have years."

The old man smiled, showing his black and brown teeth. "So do I," he said. "Follow me!"

Edmond slid into the tunnel and wriggled like a worm through the narrow space. He rose into another cell, as dark and dingy as his own.

The old man bowed. "My name is Abbé Faria."

"Abbé?" Edmond said. That meant priest. "Why are you in prison?"

"Because I knew a secret that I wouldn't tell the King."

"What secret?"

The old man smiled again. "It's a secret," he said.

Then he tapped one of the stones in his cell wall. "If we dig this way for about five years, we should come out near the sea." He handed Edmond a tool made from a bent iron bed leg.

"Let's get started."

That first night, they barely dug an inch into the wall. But each night after, Edmond crawled from his cell and they continued scraping at the rock. As they dug, Edmond told the Abbé about Mercedes, and his hunger for revenge on Fernand and Danglars. But whenever he asked about the Abbé's secret, the priest just smiled and kept digging.

Each night they met, and each night the tunnel grew longer. Then, around twenty years after Edmond was thrown into Chateau D'If, the Abbé called excitedly from the end of the tunnel. "Edmond, I see daylight!"

Edmond's heart raced. They had reached the end. But as he scurried closer, the tunnel walls began to tremble. Zigzag cracks splintered along the roof.

"Abbé!" Edmond cried. "Come back."

But it was too late. Rocks crashed down as the tunnel collapsed.

Chapter 5
Escape from Chateau D'If

Heavy rocks rained down on Edmond as he struggled back through the collapsing tunnel. He managed to grab hold of the Abbé's legs and drag the old priest back to his cell. The Abbé's eyes rolled. He was badly hurt.

"I'll call the guards," Edmond said.

But the Abbé held him back. "No," he said weakly. "Listen to me…"

The Abbé pointed a shaky finger at a stone on the wall. "Look behind that stone."

Confused, Edmond dug his fingers around the edges of the rock. It was loose. Pulling it away, he found a scrap of paper. "A map?"

"Of the island of Monte Cristo," the Abbé explained. "It shows where treasure is buried. This, Edmond, is my secret. And now that I die, the treasure is yours."

The Abbé slumped to the floor. He was dead.

Tears stung Edmond's eyes. Was he now doomed to die alone in this place? He heard footsteps and dived back into the tunnel to his cell. He lay in the dark, listening to the guards discover the priest's body.

"Old fool," one of them said. "Looks like he died trying to escape. What shall we do with the body?"

"Wrap it up," another replied. "We'll get rid of it tonight."

The guards left. Cautiously, Edmond rose from the tunnel. The Abbé's body lay covered in a sack on the floor. Suddenly Edmond knew how he could escape.

Moving fast, he pulled the sack from the Abbé and dragged the body down into the tunnel. Then he rushed back and wrapped the sack around himself instead. He had the Abbé's map in his pocket, along with his digging knife. He'd let the guards bury him outside the prison, and then dig himself free.

After several hours, the guards returned. Edmond's heart hammered so hard, he was sure it would give him away, as the guards picked him up and carried him from the cell.

"He's heavy for an old man," muttered one.

Edmond heard a door creak open. For the first time in twenty years, he breathed fresh air. He was outside. Through a hole in the sack, he glimpsed the edge of the cliffs. Where were the guards going to bury him?

One of the men grabbed Edmond's leg and lashed a rope around his ankles. To Edmond's horror, he saw a cannonball attached to the other end. He realized now what was happening. The guards weren't going to bury him at all. Instead, they picked him up... and flung him off the cliff!

Chapter 6
The fisherman's replies

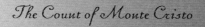

Edmond plunged into the icy water.
He wriggled free of the
sack, but he was dragged
deeper by the cannonball
attached to his legs. He felt as if
his lungs were on fire.

Then he remembered – the
knife! He grabbed the blade
from his pocket and cut the rope,
freeing himself of the weight.

He burst to the surface, but
now a wave slammed him against a
fishing boat tethered to the rocks.
Exhausted, Edmond just managed
to cling onto the side of the boat
and haul himself up onto the deck.

But there was no time to rest. Soon the guards would discover his escape. With his last gasps of strength, Edmond rowed until Chateau D'If was just a shadowy speck in the distance.

Ahead, he could see lights glimmering on Marseilles' docks. Edmond had dreamed of his home for twenty years, but the sight gave him no joy. All he thought of was revenge.

Another fishing boat passed. "I am headed to Marseilles to surprise an old friend," Edmond called. "Do you know a man named Danglars?"

"I did once," the fisherman replied. "But he moved to Paris. I hear he is a rich banker now, called Baron Danglars."

"What about Fernand Mondego?"

"He too is a rich man. He lives in Paris with his wife and son Albert."

Edmond couldn't believe it. While he had been rotting in jail, his enemies had grown rich. "Do you know a girl named Mercedes?" he asked.

"You are truly out of luck," the fisherman said. "She lives in Paris too. She is Fernand's wife."

Edmond slumped to the deck. More than ever, he craved revenge. A plan was forming in his head. First he would go to Monte Cristo and find the Abbé's treasure. Then he would disguise himself as a rich noble like his enemies. He would enter their lives. And he would destroy them.

Chapter 7
The carnival at Rome

Almost one year after Edmond's escape from prison, a carriage clattered up to the most magnificent hotel in Rome. Two young men stepped out. One was Beauchamp, a writer from Paris. The other was Albert Mondego, the son of Mercedes and Fernand.

"This is the finest hotel in Rome!" Albert declared. "Surely it is the perfect place to watch the carnival." But inside, his smile disappeared.

"I'm afraid all of our rooms have been taken," the hotel manager said. "By one man."

"What sort of man would take over an entire hotel?" asked Beauchamp.

Albert was already marching upstairs to find out. He had boasted to his friends about staying here, and would look a fool if he could not. A door flew open in front of him as he passed.

"Gentlemen," said a servant, bowing before them, "the Count of Monte Cristo is expecting you."

"Expecting us?" Albert said. "What a peculiar thing."

Inside, the room was decorated like a palace, with tapestries on the walls and magnificent paintings in golden frames. Albert had never seen such luxury.

"My father knows all of Europe's noblemen," he told Beauchamp, "but I've never heard of the Count of Monte Cristo. Who is this man?"

A door flew open and in swept Edmond Dantes. His face was disguised by a neat beard and he wore a velvet cloak, intricately embroidered with gold. He

introduced himself as the Count of Monte Cristo.

"Gentlemen," the Count said, bowing gracefully, "I hoped you would join me to watch the carnival from my balcony."

As the Count led the way, Albert whispered to Beauchamp. "How mysterious! His skin is as white as snow. It is as if he has been living underground."

Fireworks fizzed into the sky and the carnival began. As costumed performers paraded through the streets, the Count charmed Albert and Beauchamp with tales of his travels around the world.

"But it is Paris that I would most like to visit," he said.

"My dear Count," Albert said. "I live in Paris! You *must* come and visit."

"I would love to," said the Count. "Can you recommend a banker in the city to look after my money?"

"There is none finer than Baron Danglars," Albert replied. "And you can meet my father too, Fernand Mondego."

A muscle twitched in the Count's neck. "Perfect," he said. "I will come in exactly one month, at three o'clock."

As more fireworks exploded over the balcony, Albert leaned to Beauchamp. "What a magnificent man!" he whispered. "I cannot wait for him to meet my parents."

Chapter 8

Paris

Exactly one month later, at precisely three o'clock, the doorbell rang at Albert's home in Paris. The Count of Monte Cristo was waiting, dressed immaculately.

"My dear Count," Albert said. "I had begun to think our meeting in Rome was a dream."

Albert led the Count into the drawing room, where two men rose and bowed.

"My father," Albert said, "Fernand Mondego. And Baron Danglars, the richest banker in Paris."

The Count's pale face flushed red as he came face to face with the men who ruined his life. They didn't recognize him, but he knew them immediately. Danglars had the same pompous sneer on his face, while Fernand remained a gloomy figure, despite the golden military medals on his coat.

"Those are fine medals," the Count said.

Fernand puffed out his chest. "I won them defending a fortress against Turks in Greece."

"My father made his fortune while in Greece," Albert added eagerly.

"And what happened to the fortress?"

"I am afraid that it was lost."

Danglars poured the Count a glass of champagne. The baron glanced greedily at the Count's emerald rings. "Albert tells me that you require the services of a banker," he said. "My customers have accounts with me of over a million francs."

"A million francs?" said the Count, laughing.
"Why ever would I need a bank for such a trifling sum?
I have two million in my pocket right now."

Danglars was lost for words. The Count spoke so
simply he was either telling the truth or he was mad.
But before he could ask which, a door opened and a
woman entered dressed in a flowing silk gown.

It was Mercedes. She saw the Count and froze.
Her mouth cracked open and a tiny gasp came out.

"Are you ill Mother?" Albert asked. "You look suddenly pale."

The Count simply bowed. "It is a look that suits you well madame," he said. "And now that I have met you, I am afraid I must leave. I only came to invite you all to a party at my new house in Paris."

The Count smiled and left. But inside his carriage, he groaned. Had Mercedes recognized him? It was strange seeing her after so long. He felt no love, only hatred for Fernand and Danglars. He might have killed them right then, but death was too good for them. He planned to make them suffer...

Chapter 9
The Count's party

For the next few weeks, only one name interested anyone in Paris society – the Count of Monte Cristo. At plays, operas and dinners, everyone asked about this mysterious man and his magnificent wealth.

As if to answer, the Count threw a lavish party at his new house. All the richest nobles arrived, stylishly dressed and dripping with jewels. But everyone's eyes were on the Count, as he moved gracefully among his guests.

None of the guests studied their host closer than Mercedes. As the Count passed, she took his arm. "It is hot in here, Count. Perhaps you would take a walk with me in the garden?"

For a second, the Count's calm smile vanished and panic flashed across his face. Mercedes took his arm and they strolled among elegant fountains and lime trees hung with twinkling Chinese lanterns.

"Albert tells me that you have sailed all over the world, Count," Mercedes said. "I wonder if you ever met a sailor named Edmond Dantes?"

The Count flinched. "I have not madame. Is he a friend?"

"He was a man I loved. But I was told that he died in prison, many years ago."

The Count flinched again. His jaw clenched. "Who told you that?" he demanded.

But before Mercedes could reply, Danglars interrupted their walk. "Excuse me Count," he asked, "but I wonder if you have given any thought to my services as a banker?"

The Count turned. He looked at Danglars with awful calmness. "Very well Baron," he said, "the time has come. Follow me."

The Count led Danglars into his drawing room, where he opened a wooden chest. "I would like you to look after my entire fortune."

Danglars' eyes glinted with greed. The chest was filled with diamonds, rubies and emeralds that glimmered like a rainbow in the gaslight.

"Can you take them to your bank immediately?" asked the Count.

Without another word, Danglars picked up the chest and carried it from the room.

The Count smiled grimly. His plan for revenge had begun. "Your greed ruined my life Danglars," he said to himself. "Now watch as it ruins your own."

Chapter 10
The Roman catacombs

It wasn't the weight of the Count's treasure that made Danglars' arms tremble. It was excitement. He had hoped to become the Count's banker, but now he had a new idea. He would steal the Count's fortune! "Take me to Rome!" he called to his driver.

The carriage rode for hours. Danglars dozed and dreamed about how he would spend the Count's treasure. At last they came to a sign pointing to Rome. But the carriage turned in the other direction.

"Driver," Danglars called, "we are going the wrong way."

The carriage didn't turn. Danglars glimpsed a hooded figure in the driver's

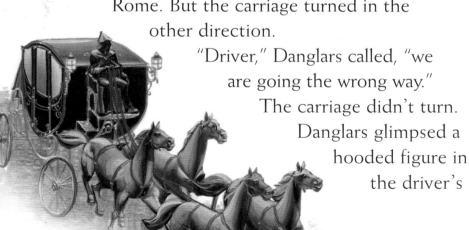

seat – a bandit? Had he been kidnapped?

The carriage finally stopped and the door creaked open. The hooded man aimed a pistol at Danglars. "Get out," he said.

Danglars climbed from the carriage, clutching the Count's treasure. They had reached the Roman catacombs, underground tombs cut deep into the rock. The hooded man pushed Danglars through a dank passage and into a cramped cell. A door slammed shut behind him.

Danglars sat in dismal darkness, confused. Why hadn't the bandit taken the treasure?

After several hours, he banged on the door. "At least bring me some food!" he cried.

The door creaked open. The hooded man placed a plate of succulent roast chicken on the floor. Danglars reached for it greedily, but the hooded man raised his pistol.

"This meal costs ten diamonds," he said.

Danglars hesitated. Ten diamonds! It was ridiculous, but he had no food and all of the Count's treasure. He threw the man the jewels and pounced on the plate. "But you'll get no more jewels from me!" he warned.

Danglars was wrong. He resisted for as long as he could, but eventually his hunger got the better of him. He paid ten emeralds for roast beef, and then fifty rubies just for water.

After several days, he had only three diamonds left. Two days passed and Danglars didn't eat. He grew weak and desperately hungry. He sank to his knees, clutching his aching stomach. "Why do you make me suffer?" he pleaded.

The door opened. The hooded man stepped inside the cell. "Suffer?" he said. "There are men who have suffered worse."

"No," Danglars groaned, "there are none."

"I will show you one," the hooded man replied. Slowly, he peeled back his hood and revealed his face.

"The Count of Monte Cristo!" Danglars cried.

The Count grabbed Danglars' collar. His eyes were red and wild with rage. "No!" he seethed. "I am the man whose life you ruined twenty years ago. I am Edmond Dantes!"

Danglars fell back in horror, sobbing.

"Now your life is ruined too," said the Count, as he took the last jewels from his chest and strode from the cell. "Fernand," he whispered, "you are next..."

Chapter 11
Challenge at the opera

Two days later in Paris, Albert Mondego stormed into the office of his friend Beauchamp. He waved a newspaper at the journalist. "Have you read this?"

Beauchamp's face darkened as he read the report. The newspaper called Albert's father a traitor. It claimed to have evidence proving that, years ago, Fernand surrendered a Greek fortress to enemy Turks for money. That was how Fernand made his fortune.

"Where is your father now?" said Beauchamp.

"Soldiers are searching for him all over Paris," Albert replied. "You have friends at this paper, Beauchamp. Find out what evidence they have."

Soon after, Beauchamp returned. "The newspaper received a document," he told Albert, a worried frown on his face. "It is the contract agreeing the surrender of the fortress to the Turks. Albert, it's signed by your father."

"It is a fraud!" Albert insisted. "Some unknown enemy is acting against my father."

"Not unknown," Beauchamp said. "My friend at the newspaper knew exactly who gave him the document. Albert, it was the Count of Monte Cristo!"

The pair raced to the Paris Opera House, where Albert knew the Count would be that

evening. He stormed down the aisle, to where the Count sat sipping champagne.

"I demand an explanation," Albert said.

"An explanation?" the Count replied. "At the opera? Surely this is not the place, my friend."

"You are no friend of mine, Count. Are you an enemy of my father?"

A gasp echoed around the stalls. Everyone watched as the Count rose. His glare was so fierce that Albert stepped back in fright.

"I am," the Count said.

"I demand to know why," Albert replied.

"I cannot tell you."

"Then I challenge you to a duel. We will meet tomorrow morning with pistols. Good day sir!" With that, Albert turned and strode away.

The Count straightened his coat and returned to his seat, as if he wasn't remotely bothered by Albert's attack. But he was. He *had* given the document to the newspaper, but in the hope that Fernand would be the one to challenge him. Perhaps, though, this was a better revenge. He had planned to kill Fernand. But if Fernand wouldn't fight, he would kill his son instead.

On stage, the curtain rose and the final act began.

Chapter 12
Duel in the park

BOOM!
The blast from the Count's pistol echoed around the park, scattering pigeons from the trees. The shot hit the trunk dead in the middle. The Count's aim was perfect.

The Count rubbed his tired eyes. He hadn't slept at all last night. He had come here to punish Fernand by killing his son. But he felt a sadness... Was he doing the right thing?

A carriage approached, and Albert stepped out
with Beauchamp. His eyes were red and puffy and
his pistol trembled in his hand. He had clearly not
slept either.

"Count," he said, "tell me what cause you have to
hate my father."

"I cannot."

"Then we must fight."

Beauchamp stood between the two men.
"Gentlemen," he instructed, "you must each take ten
paces and then turn and fire."

The duel began.

The Count raised his pistol and began pacing. *One... two...* He thought about his life before Chateau D'If, and the man he once was. Happy Edmond Dantes... *Four... five...* He thought of Fernand, and how he had stolen that happiness. *Seven... eight...* The Count's finger curled around the trigger. *Nine... ten!* The Count turned.

"EDMOND!"

The Count froze. Mercedes raced across the park. Tears streamed down her cheeks. "Edmond!" she gasped. "Please spare my son!"

But the Count's pistol remained fixed on Albert. "Edmond is dead," he said coldly. "I am simply an angel of vengeance."

"But why Edmond? Why do you seek revenge? Fernand has done nothing to you."

The Count's whole body trembled with rage. "Nothing?" he cried. "Because of him, I rotted in jail for twenty years."

"No," Mercedes said, "not Fernand..."

"You do not believe me? Here is the proof!"

The Count pulled a crumpled paper from his pocket and threw it to Mercedes. It was the same letter that, twenty years ago, accused him of treason. Only then, the soldiers had hidden the signatures at the bottom. One of them said Danglars. The other belonged to...

"Fernand Mondego," Mercedes whispered.

Her legs buckled and she fell weeping to the
long grass.

Albert read the letter too. His pistol slipped
from his hand. But still the Count kept his
weapon aimed at Albert's head. His hand
shook. He gazed at Mercedes, crying at
his feet. Slowly, he lowered the pistol.

"Edmond," Mercedes sobbed.

"No," the Count said softly.
"I do not know who
I am anymore..."

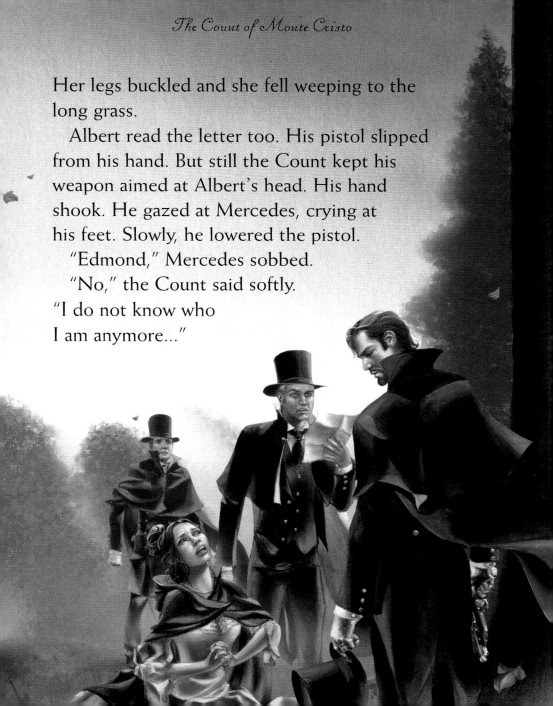

Chapter 13
Wait and hope

Fernand Mondego jumped breathlessly over the fence and into the back garden of his house. He hid in the shadows, making sure he hadn't been seen. His darkest secrets were now public, and he was hunted by the army. If he was caught, he would surely hang.

He crept into his house and hurriedly filled a case with clothes. He planned to flee to Marseilles and then hide on a boat to Africa.

Just then, he heard footsteps. Fernand watched through a crack in the door as Mercedes and Albert came down the stairs. They too carried bags. And they were with the Count of Monte Cristo.

"Come Mother," Albert said, "this is no longer our home."

The words stabbed like a knife in Fernand's heart. He had lost everything! But then he heard something even worse. As Mercedes left, she turned to the Count and said, "Thank you Edmond."

Fernand sunk to the floor. The Count of Monte Cristo was Edmond Dantes!

There was a loud knock on the back door. Soldiers gathered in the garden. They had seen Fernand inside, but Fernand was too stunned to move. Even as they smashed down the door, he just curled on the floor, muttering the name of the man who had ruined him... "Edmond... Edmond Dantes..."

The Count walked Mercedes and Albert to their carriage. He heard the commotion inside the house, but he didn't care. His obsession with revenge had already gone too far, almost killing poor Albert. It was over. He never wanted to hear the name Fernand Mondego again. Neither did Mercedes or Albert. They were moving to Italy, far from the scandal that had shamed their family.

"You could come with us," Mercedes said, as the Count helped her into the carriage.

But the Count just smiled. He took her hand and kissed it gently. "I cannot," he said. "I have lived all this time for revenge. Now, I must live for something new. I will find a new life."

As the carriage rattled away, Mercedes leaned from the window. "Edmond, how do you know that you will find this new life?"

The Count closed his eyes, feeling the warm winter sun soothe his pale skin. "I will wait," he said. "Wait and hope."

THE PRISONER OF ZENDA

Chapter 1
On having red hair

Chapter 2
A merry evening

Chapter 3
A dilemma

Chapter 4
The Coronation

Chapter 5
In the cellar

Chapter 1
On having red hair

"When are you going to *do* something with your life, Rudolf?" said my brother's wife, Rose, while I was trying to eat breakfast. "You're old enough to get a job," she went on. "Really, you've done nothing with your life except—"

"Mess around?" I said. "What's wrong with that? I don't want a job."

My remark annoyed Rose. I stroked my dark red hair, annoying her even more.

"At least your brother's hair is black, thank goodness," she said.

"Well, I like having red hair, and I like being a Ruritanian," I said. Rose scowled.

At this point, perhaps I should explain one or two things.

Whenever I read books, I always skip the boring explanations, but I realize that I must explain why Rose hated my red hair so much, and why I sat in a London drawing room and talked about being a Ruritanian. It starts with an old family scandal...

More than two hundred years ago, a handsome prince visited the English court. He had dark red hair, and an unusually long, straight nose. The Prince fell in love with a beautiful lady and duelled with her husband to win her.

Both men were wounded in the duel.
The Prince went home to Ruritania,
where he later became King Rudolf I,
and the lady's husband died of his wounds.

Some months later, his widow gave birth
to a baby with blue eyes, an unusually long,
straight nose, and dark red hair.

In every generation in that family — that is to say, in *my* family — there is one child with red hair, and one with a long straight nose. And I just happened to have both.

"Rudolf, please listen," said Rose. "You really must find a job. I know of one that starts in September," she added, and looked at me so sweetly I gave in.

"Fine," I said, "I'll do it." I had given her my promise, and I would stick to it. But I had six months of freedom left. I would use the time to travel to Ruritania and discover the land of my red-haired ancestors.

Chapter 2

A merry evening

I arrived in Ruritania to find the place in a state of great excitement. A new king was to be crowned the next day. I decided to go to the capital, Streslau, to watch and stopped off in the sleepy town of Zenda on my way.

It was a bright, sunny morning, and I went for a stroll through the forest. After walking an hour or two, I sat against a tree and drifted to sleep. I was in the middle of a pleasant dream, when a rough, loud voice woke me up.

"By the devil! Shave his beard and he'd be the King!"

I opened my eyes. Two men stood over me. One was short and stout, with a bristly moustache and pale blue eyes. The other was much younger, with dark hair and a graceful, handsome face.

I scrambled to my feet.

"He's just the right height too!" muttered the older man, staring at me. He reached forwards to shake my hand. "I'm Colonel Sapt, and this is Fritz," he said. "We're servants of the King of Ruritania. May I ask... who are you?"

"Rudolf Rassendyll from England," I said.

"Rassendyll, Rassendyll," muttered Colonel Sapt. His face lit up. "By Heaven! Fritz, you know the old story, don't you?"

At that moment, a voice called out from the woods behind us. "Fritz? Where are you?"

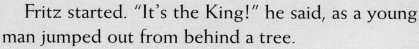

The Prisoner of Zenda

Fritz started. "It's the King!" he said, as a young man jumped out from behind a tree.

When I saw him, I gasped. Seeing me, he turned pale. For a moment we both stood still. Apart from my beard, and a couple of inches in height, the King and I could have been twins. We gazed at each other, astonished. Then I bowed respectfully.

"Who is this gentleman?" the bewildered King asked Colonel Sapt. Sapt whispered in the King's ear. The King frowned, then started to smile. Finally, he burst out laughing. "Cousin!" he said, slapping me on the back. "You must forgive me for being so startled. Where are you headed?"

"To the coronation," I said.

The King laughed again. "I can't wait to see my brother's face when he sees the pair of us. Well, you shall stay with us at the hunting lodge tonight."

And so, that evening I dined with Rudolf, the King of Ruritania. We ate heartily, drank much and talked merrily.

When dinner was over, Josef, the King's servant, set a dusty old flagon on the table. "His Royal Highness, Michael, Duke of Streslau, sends you this wine with his love."

"Well, well," said the King grimly. "Does my brother think I'll be too scared to drink? Open it up! Friends," he continued, "you may have anything I own. But don't ask me for a single drop of this wine.

I'll drink it all, to the health of that sly knave, my brother Black Michael."

With that, he gulped the wine down to the last drop. He laid his head on his arms, and that is all I can remember of the evening.

Chapter 3
A dilemma

The next morning I awoke with a start and a shiver. I was soaking wet, and Sapt was standing in front of me, holding an empty bucket. I jumped up.

"What are you doing?" I shouted.

"Nothing else would wake you," said Sapt. "Look."

In front of me the King lay stretched out on the floor. His face was as red as his hair, and he was snoring loudly. Sapt gave him a hard kick, but it made no difference.

"We've been trying to wake him for an hour," said Fritz.

I felt for the King's pulse. It was very slow. "Do you think that last bottle was drugged?" I asked.

"Yes, and by his brother, Black Michael," Sapt said, through gritted teeth. He knelt beside the

King and put a hand on his back more gently. "Everyone knows Black Michael wants the throne," he went on, "and he'd give his soul to marry Princess Flavia, who's to be Queen."

"He'll never make it to the coronation. And if he isn't crowned today, he'll never be crowned," Fritz added.

"Why not?" I asked.

"The whole army will be at the coronation, with Black Michael at its head," said Sapt. "If King Rudolf isn't crowned today, Michael will be King before tomorrow."

For a moment we were all silent.

Then Sapt took his pipe from his mouth and turned to me. "As a man grows old he believes in Fate," he said. "Fate brought you here. Fate now sends you to Streslau to be crowned."

"Impossible," I muttered. "Everyone would know it was me!"

"If you shave your beard, you'd never be discovered," said Sapt. "I think you're scared."

"The King can rest here today," said Fritz. "By tomorrow he'll have recovered. He can return to the palace, and you can continue with your travels."

"But—"

"Of course, we'll die if we're found out," said Sapt. "But I'd rather die than let that knave, Black Michael, steal the throne. And he will, if you don't help."

The clock ticked fifty or sixty times. Then my face must have changed, because Sapt looked relieved.

"So, you'll go?"

I nodded. I didn't seem to have a choice.

Chapter 4
The Coronation

"Long live King Rudolf!" came a shout.
Every house was hung with flags, and the streets were packed with cheering crowds. Ladies stood on balconies, scattering roses before my horse. I was at the head of a grand procession, and perhaps I should have been terrified, but I was giddy with excitement. For a moment, I almost thought I really was the King.

"He's taller than I thought," someone said.

"And more handsome," said another voice. (It was all just flattery, I'm sure.)

Soon the great oak doors of Streslau cathedral stood before me. For the first time, I realized the sheer madness of what I was doing. Everything was in a mist as I walked up the aisle. Only two faces stood out: the face of a pale and beautiful girl, who was gazing at me, and the face of a man with red cheeks, black hair, and dark, deep eyes.

When he saw me, his jaw dropped and the helmet in his hands fell to the floor with a crash. He stared at me with hatred in his eyes.

"So that's Black Michael," I thought.

I knelt to receive the crown, and, moments later, I stepped outside with the beautiful girl by my side. The crowds broke into wild applause.

"Her Royal Highness the Princess Flavia!" shouted a herald.

"When's the wedding?" someone yelled, as we stepped up into a carriage. As it rattled off down the street, the Princess turned to me.

"You know Rudolf, you look quite different today."

"Really?" I said. Her remark wasn't that surprising. But it was alarming.

"You look more thoughtful, and I'm sure you're thinner," she went on. "You look almost like a different person. Surely you haven't begun to take anything seriously?"

"Would that make you happy?" I asked, desperately trying to think of a way to change the subject.

"You know my views," she replied.

It would have been handy if I did know her views. I wished I knew a single thing about her, and I secretly cursed myself for not asking Sapt what on earth I should say to her.

"Well, go on, silly," said Flavia.

"Um, what was that?"

"Go on, wave!" Flavia said. "Or have you quite forgotten how to be a king?"

As I waved to the crowds, the Princess turned to me. I realized I had never seen anyone so beautiful. She whispered into my ear: "Be careful of Michael! You must keep watch on him. He wants—"

"He wants the throne that I have," I said, "and the Princess I hope to win."

Flavia blushed, and I thought I was playing the King's part very well.

Guns fired and trumpets blared. We had arrived at the palace. That night, as I sat at the head of a state banquet, I wondered what the real King was doing.

Chapter 5

In the cellar

As darkness fell, Fritz, Sapt and I slipped out of of the palace, and rode to Zenda to get the King and bring him back to Streslau. But when we arrived at the hunting lodge, no one came to greet us. Inside, all was quiet. As Sapt walked along a corridor, he swore loudly. From under the cellar door, a red stain had spread over the floor and dried there.

Sapt sank against the wall. I tried the door. It was locked.

"Where's the King?" I said. I took my pistol, fired at the lock and the door swung open. Holding a candle above my head, I walked inside. I could see several bottles of wine, spiders crawling all over the walls, and, in the middle of the room, the body of a man lying flat on his back, with a red slit across his throat.

I knelt down and saw that it was the King's servant, Josef. I heard a shout and turned to see Sapt behind me, his eyes full of terror.

"The King? My God, the King!" he cried.

The candle's light stretched to every corner of the cellar. "The King is not here," I said.

For ten minutes or more we sat in silence, before old Sapt stamped his foot on the floor, and was himself again. "Black Michael must have the King," he declared.

"We must find every soldier in Streslau," said Fritz, "and attack him as soon as we can."

"Come on! Let's go to Streslau!" I said.

But old Sapt pulled out his pipe and lit it carefully, and a smile appeared on his wrinkled face. "That's right, lad," he said, "We'll go back to Streslau. The King shall be in the capital again tomorrow. The *crowned* King."

"You're crazy!" I said.

"We have to go," said Sapt. "If we return and tell people the trick we played, what do you think they'll do?"

"But Black Michael knows I'm a fake!"

"Of course," replied Sapt. "But he can hardly say, 'This isn't the King, because I've kidnapped him,' can he?"

"If you pretend to be the King, you may still save him," said Fritz.

It was a wild plan, but I knew I had been offered a chance I would never have again.

"Sapt," I said, "I'll do it."

Chapter 6
An adventure with a tea table

A king may have a hard life, but a man pretending to be a king has a harder one. The next day, Sapt told me my duties, my likes and dislikes. He told me that the King liked white wine and dogs, and hated cats and too much salt. There were a thousand rules to remember, and I soon forgot them all.

The only reason I wasn't caught was that no one imagined that anyone could do something so dangerous and stupid as impersonate a king. No one except Black Michael, who paid me a visit that very day.

"Your Majesty," he said, with a smile on his lips and a murderous look in his eyes.

"Dear brother," I said, "how kind of you to send me that bottle of wine. It gave me so much energy for the coronation."

"I'm glad," said Michael. "Your good health is always my first concern."

"How lucky I am to have such a loyal brother," I observed.

"I have a friend who would like to meet you," Michael said. "A loyal servant of the King: Rupert Hentzau."

A handsome young man strolled into the room, and gave me an insolent smile.

"He's in on the secret too," I thought.

When I was finally rid of them both, I turned to Sapt. "Who was that?"

"Rupert Hentzau is Black Michael's bravest soldier, and the best sword fighter in the country," he replied. "He has two hobbies. The first is falling in love with beautiful women..."

"And the other?" I asked.

"Defeating his enemies. He'll be happy to cut your throat just as soon as he gets the chance."

So now I had not one deadly enemy, but two.

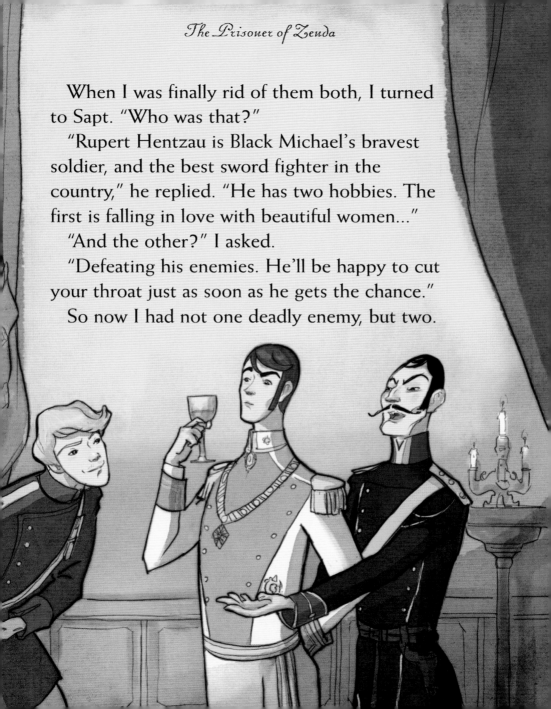

The next evening, Sapt walked into my dressing room and threw a letter on the table.

> *To the King,*
> *At the end of New Avenue, there is a house with a large garden. In the garden is a summer house. Wait there at midnight, and you will find a faithful friend who can tell you news of great importance.*
> *Antoinette*

"Who's Antoinette?" I asked him.

"Black Michael's sweetheart," Sapt replied. "If Michael becomes King, he'll marry Princess Flavia. Antoinette will do anything to stop him from taking the throne – so she can keep Black Michael for herself. But make no mistake," he went on, "this letter is a trap. If you go, you'll never get out of the garden alive."

"Perhaps. But I believe her, and I will go."

"It'll be the death of you," said Sapt.

"I'll go, or go back to England," I said.

"So be it," said Sapt with a sigh.

Thus, at midnight, we arrived at the house.

"I'll wait here," he said. "If I hear a shot—"

"Run away," I said. "There's no point in us both being killed."

Sapt waited with the horses, while I crept into the garden, my revolver ready. A large building loomed in front of me. I climbed some steps and pushed open the door.

"Shut the door," came a whisper. A beautiful woman stood in the darkness. "I know what you are doing, Mr. Rassendyll," she hissed. "In twenty minutes three men will be here to kill you. You must be gone by then. Michael plans to kill you, murder the King and marry Princess Flavia."

"Where's the King now?" I asked.

"In his castle at Zenda. When you cross the drawbridge, you come to... What's that?"

There were footsteps outside.

"They're here too soon," she hissed.

"Rassendyll," came a voice. It was Rupert Hentzau. "Let us in. We have an offer for you. We won't shoot."

I peered through a chink in the door. Three revolvers pointed at it.

"What's your offer?" I asked.

"We'll take you safely to the frontier, and give you fifty thousand pounds, if you promise never to return."

"I accept," I said. "Let me out, and I promise not to fire before you do."

In the bare summer house was a small, iron tea table. I picked it up. When I turned it on its side, it made a fine shield for my head and body.

"Stand back," I ordered Antoinette quietly. "Gentlemen," I said more loudly, "if you would open the door?"

I smiled as the door swung open. With a shout, I charged through. Three shots rang out and battered my shield. The table crashed into the three men, and they and I and the brave tea table all tumbled down

the steps of the summerhouse.

"Ha!" I jumped to my feet as a shot whizzed past my ear. Black Michael and Rupert Hentzau lay in a tangle under the tea table, and another soldier lay sprawled on his back.

Rupert raised his revolver and fired again. I fired back, and raced away like a hare. I tore back to where Sapt was still waiting and clapped him on the back. "Let's go home, old man," I said with a laugh.

"You're safe!" he cried. "And what on earth is so funny?"

"I beat them with a tea table!" I said, jumping up on to my horse.

As we rode away, I felt particularly proud because I'd kept my promise, and not fired before they did.

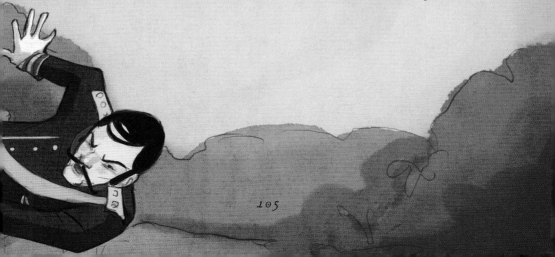

Chapter 7
A grand ball

"We must go straight to Zenda," I said to Sapt the next morning.

"The preparations are all made," said Sapt. "But there's one more thing you must do as King. I've arranged for you to give a ball for Princess Flavia tonight. You must ask her to marry you. The people desire it."

"I won't!" I said. "I refuse to make a fool of her. How could I trick her? What happens when

the real King returns?"

Sapt said nothing. But he knew I would obey him, despite my protests, for I had fallen in love with the Princess.

That night, as I danced a waltz with Flavia, curious eyes and eager whispers surrounded us.

Afterwards, we wandered together into a little room. Stammering, I told her I loved her. Her reply took me by surprise.

"How is it that I love you now, Rudolf? I... I never did before you were crowned."

I was filled with happiness. She loved me – not the King!

"Why are you so happy to hear that I didn't love you before?" she said, laughing.

"If I were not the King," I said, "if I were only a private gentleman..."

Flavia put her hand in mine. "If you were a convict in Streslau prison, I'd still love you," she said, her eyes shining with happiness.

"Flavia," I blurted out, "I am not the K–"

"Beg your pardon, sir," said a gruff voice. Sapt's face appeared at the window. "The cardinal wishes to say goodnight to you."

I caught the angry look in his eyes. I do not know how long he had been standing there, but he had come just in time.

Chapter 8
A desperate plan

The next morning I set out for Zenda, with Sapt, Fritz, and ten strong men. We stayed in a fine house in the woods, close to Black Michael's castle.

Sapt went out riding and came back with a triumphant look in his eyes. He'd paid a servant – Johann – to tell him where the King was.

"At the end of the bridge in the castle gatehouse, there are two rooms cut into the stone," he said. "The outer room has two guards. The King is held in chains in the inner room."

"Does the King's room have a window?" I asked.

"The window is filled with a pipe, just big enough to fit a body into," Sapt answered.

"If an attacker reaches the outer room, one guard will fight him off. The other will murder the King and send his body down the pipe. The pipe leads into the moat. The King's body will never be found."

Sapt turned pale. "The King is very sick," he added. "A doctor is being held prisoner with him in his cell. He can barely walk, or speak. I'm afraid he may not live long..."

For a while, we sat in bewildered silence.

"It's a hard nut to crack," Sapt finished. "But we must attack tonight."

"I think I have an idea," I replied. "Is Antoinette in the castle?"

"She is," said Sapt.

"Then I hope she'll help us. Our lives may depend on it." I scribbled a note to Antoinette and gave it to Johann.

> Antoinette ~
> At midnight, call out for Black Michael.
> Say that Rupert Hentzau is attacking you.
> It's our only chance to save the King.
> Rudolf

If all went to plan, Johann would let Sapt into the castle after nightfall. Then, when Antoinette called for help, Black Michael would come running and fall into the murderous arms of Sapt. Meanwhile, I would try to rescue the King.

Chapter 9
Attack!

In darkness, our party set out for the castle. Sapt and I rode first, with ten soldiers following us. We clung to shadows, and rode as quietly as we could. When we arrived, Sapt knocked very lightly on the door. The servant, Johann opened it, and Sapt and the others slipped inside.

I decided to stay outside and keep watch. Crouching down by the gatehouse, I prepared for a long wait.

The clock struck twelve, then one, then a light shone through a window.

"Help! Michael, help!" came a cry, followed by a shriek of pure terror.

I was tingling in every nerve.

"What's the matter?" roared Black Michael. "I'm coming up!"

"Help, Michael, it's Rupert Hentzau!" screamed Antoinette.

Sapt should be striking Black Michael now, I thought. But a moment later, I saw Black Michael still upright in Antoinette's bedroom. My heart sank. What had happened to Sapt?

I heard Black Michael shout, "What's going on? Where is he?" There were running footsteps and then Black Michael shouted again. "Rupert, you sly dog! How could you attack Antoinette?"

Then Rupert's voice: "I did no such thing!"

"Ha! Do you expect me to believe that?"

I heard the clash of crossed swords as the two men began to fight.

"Come on Michael," said Rupert and Black Michael cried out.

The next thing I knew, Rupert had
jumped onto a windowsill, laughing
and waving his sword in his hand.

Blood was pouring down his face. He
laughed again as he flung himself headlong
into the moat.

As Rupert jumped, a guard peered out of the door beside me.

"What's going on?" he said.

I struck him with all the strength I had. He fell without a word, and I knelt beside him.

"The keys! The keys!" I muttered, rifling through his pockets. At last I had them. Seizing the largest key, I tried it in the lock of the door that led to the King's prison, and found myself at the top of a flight of stone steps.

I took a lantern from the wall, and stood still for a moment, listening.

"Who the devil can that be?" I heard a voice say. It came from behind the door at the bottom of the stairs.

Another voice hissed: "Shall we kill him?"

I strained to hear the answer, and I could have cried with relief when it came.

"Wait a bit. There'll be trouble if we strike too soon."

There was a moment's silence. I heard the bolt of

the door being drawn back and put out the
lantern at once.

"It's dark, do you have a light?" said a voice.

I rushed down the stairs...

...and flung myself through the door, sword in hand.

Two guards stood before me. One staggered backwards while the other drew his sword.

"Ha!" I cried, and rushed madly at one of the guards. I drove him against the wall.

He fought bravely, but he was no great swordsman, and in a moment he lay on the floor before me.

I spun around, but the other guard was gone. He had rushed into the King's room, slammed the door behind him, and even now was at work, inside. He would have killed the King, and perhaps me too, had it not been for one brave man.

When I forced the door open, the King was standing in the corner of the room. I barely recognized him. His chained hands were at his sides, and he was laughing like a lunatic. The guard and the King's doctor were struggling in the middle of the room.

The doctor had no weapon to defend himself and all too soon he was backed up against the wall with nowhere to go.

With a cry of triumph, the guard drove his
sword through the poor doctor, and turned to me.
    We fought sword to sword: silently, sternly and
hard. He knew more tricks than I did and a smile
flickered across his face as his sword cut deep into
my arm.

I know he would have killed me, for
he was the best swordsman I had ever
fought, but as he pressed me to the wall,
the lunatic of a King in the corner
jumped up, shouting.

"It's cousin Rudolf! I'll help you!"
Picking up a chair, he staggered over
to us.

"Strike his legs, Sire!"
I encouraged him.

With an oath, the guard swung around. He made a fierce swipe at the King, who fell to the floor with a cry. The guard turned back to me, but stepped in a pool of blood on the floor. For a second he slipped, and I was on him.

I drew my sword across his throat, and he fell against the doctor. Was the King dead? I rushed to his side. It seemed as if he were: there was a great cut across his forehead.

I knelt to hear if he was breathing, but as I did, I heard footsteps outside. In another second, I could be surrounded by Black Michael's men.

I took my sword and dragged myself up the stairs. Where was Sapt? Had our men taken the castle? I stood for a second, catching my breath as I tore a strip off my shirt and wrapped it around my aching, bleeding arm.

At that moment, I would have given anything to see Sapt appear.

And then I heard a laugh. It was a merry, scornful laugh – the laugh of Rupert Hentzau. Sapt and his men couldn't have taken the castle. If they had, Rupert would be dead. I ran to a window and looked out.

In the middle of the bridge stood Rupert, sword in hand. His white shirt was spattered with blood. "Michael! You dog!" he shouted. "Come out and fight me. Come out, if you wish to win Antoinette."

I watched spellbound, waiting to see what would happen. Then Sapt's voice roared from inside the castle. "Black Michael is dead!" Seconds later, Sapt himself strode onto the bridge.

Sapt walked towards Rupert, a group of his men behind him. Slowly and deliberately, he raised his revolver and took careful aim.

Rupert was trapped. He would have to rush forward to overcome Sapt and if he turned, Sapt would shoot as he ran away.

"Goodbye," Rupert said. And before Sapt had a chance to fire, Rupert bowed gracefully, and dived off the bridge into the moat once more.

I had to move quickly. To have any chance of catching him, I'd have to dive in too.

I leaped into the water and swam until my lungs were bursting. Meanwhile, Rupert had crossed the moat and climbed the wall on the other side.

"Rudolf Rassendyll, the little actor," he said, pointing his sword at my heart. If I had tried to climb up, he would have sliced me in two. "Aren't you getting cold?"

"Not at all," I replied. "It's a lovely night for a swim."

Rupert disappeared from view. When I reached the

top of the wall, he was fleeing into the forest.

I chased Rupert for what seemed like hours. When I finally caught up with him, he was leaping onto a horse.

"So, is the King dead?" he asked scornfully.

"I don't know," I said.

"You fool," he sneered, and I lunged at him with my sword.

He had the advantage of height but I managed to cut his cheek. He struck back and I rushed at him again. One or both of us would have died, but at that moment, there came a shout from behind us.

"Rudolf!" It was Fritz, my faithful friend, with a revolver in his hand.

Rupert smiled. "Goodbye, Rudolf Rassendyll," he said. He struck his horse hard with his heels, and raced away.

"Ride after him, Fritz!" I gasped.

Instead, Fritz jumped from his horse and ran to me. The blood from my wound was staining the ground.

"If you won't chase him, give me your horse, and I will," I said. I staggered to my feet, got as far as the horse, and collapsed beside it. "Is the King dead?" I gasped.

"He's alive," said Fritz, "Thanks to you."

I tried to speak, but found I could not. My eyes closed and I heard no more.

Chapter 10
Past, present, future?

And so our grand scheme was almost complete. The King was taken to a room inside the castle, where he lay recovering. We might have swapped places without anyone knowing, had it not been for Princess Flavia.

When she heard the King was hurt, she rode straight to Zenda. I knew I could never see her again. But she saw me walking through the forest with Sapt, and galloped up to us.

"Are you hurt, my love?" she called and jumped off her horse. I cast my eyes to the ground. Before I could say or do anything, she kissed me.

"Do not kiss him, your Highness," whispered Sapt. "He is not the King."

"What kind of strange joke is this?" said Flavia, laughing. "Are you telling me I don't know my own love? Rudolf!"

"He is not the King, your Highness," Sapt said again. This time, from his grave face, she knew he was not joking.

"The King is in the castle," said Sapt. "And this gentleman..."

"Look at me Rudolf!" Flavia cried. "Tell me what this means!"

I raised my eyes to look at her. "Forgive me," I said. "I am not the King."

She fell, weeping, into my arms.

That evening, Sapt told her everything. Before I left, I begged Flavia to come with me. But she refused, saying sadly, "My duty is with my country and my King."

And so I said goodbye to her, and to Zenda, for the last time.

Sapt and I rode through a night and a day, until we came to a train station just beyond the border of Ruritania. A plume of smoke was rising from a train in the distance.

"We've done well between us," I said.

"Well lad, you would have made the finest king of them all," said Sapt. "But Fate doesn't always make the right men kings."

As the train drew into the station, we embraced. I climbed aboard and was gone.

Once again, I was Rudolf Rassendyll, an Englishman with little wealth and no power.

"You've done nothing but mess around all summer," said my brother, and my sister-in-law Rose joined in.

"What a lazy boy you are. Now, about this job — it's at an embassy, in Ruritania, in Streslau."

"I won't take it," I said, immediately.

"Oh Rudolf," she sighed, "Will you never get a job?"

But I did get a job, and settled down. Now I live a quiet, simple sort of life in England.

Sometimes I wonder if I will ever again have the chance to mix in great affairs, to match my wits against my enemies, and fight a good fight. But whether my dream will come true, or is just a fancy I cannot tell.

DON
QUIXOTE

Chapter 1
Books are bad for you

Alonso Quixada had gone crazy — and quite
suddenly. The priest and the barber, who were
sitting with him in his library, sorrowfully shook
their heads.

"Too much reading!" declared the priest.

"The wrong sort of books," added the barber.
"Adventure stories indeed! And not just ordinary
ones, but tales of witches, battles, haunted castles..."

Quixada's eyes shone like candles. "Haunted
castles. *Yes!*"

"The trouble is you believe it all," said the priest. "You're really too old for stuff like that."

"And you have your housekeeper and your niece to look after you," the barber went on. "Why can't you be normal and contented like other people?"

"What a stupid question," Quixada thought, his face growing long with disgust. "It's not even worth an answer." He shoved them out of his library, sank into a chair and opened another book.

Knock, knock.

"What NOW?" he exclaimed irritably.

In marched his niece and housekeeper. The housekeeper flicked her duster over the bookshelves, sending spiders up in the air and dust down her throat. "This room's unhealthy," she choked. "Atishoo!"

"If only..." thought Quixada longingly, completely ignoring them, "if only I, too, could live like the brave knights of old."

His niece dumped a tray on a table beside him. "Such nonsense! Here's your coffee. Drink it while it's hot."

"I'll do it!" cried Quixada, kicking the coffee away. "I will! I'll be famous... immortal! Watch me right the world's wrongs, kill dragons and rescue damsels in distress."

"Don't be silly," said his niece. "Spain doesn't have dragons... and here in La Mancha there are no damsels in distress."

"Oh yes there are!" Quixada roared, and he tore up to the attic.

An ancient iron suit lay on the floor. He
scraped off the rust, cranked himself into it,
waved a cracked shield and a dented lance,
and jammed on the helmet.

"It's broken!" he mourned, but he was upset for
only a moment. Resourcefully, he found some
cardboard and made a visor, tied together with green
ribbons. Then he rushed out to his decrepit old horse.

"You," he exclaimed, "my noble steed, shall be re-named Rocinante. But hang on! I need a grand name too. I'll call myself Don Quixote de la Mancha. Now, what else do I need for my adventure? A knight with no lady-love is like a tree without leaves. Hmm..."

And then he remembered a pretty peasant girl in the village to whom he'd never spoken, called Aldonza. "I will dedicate myself to her," he decided. "And she shall be named Dulcinea del Toboso."

Rattling like a shelf of crooked saucepans, he mounted Rocinante and trotted away. "O Dulcinea, my Princess, remember me!" he murmured, as if he'd really been in love.

He rode until nightfall when, exhausted and starving, a terrible thought made him pull up his reins. Rocinante juddered to a halt. "I haven't been knighted yet! Someone must do it – and quickly!"

Don Quixote

Chapter 2
A hard day for a knight

Don Quixote had reached a dirty wayside inn where dung-spattered straw blew around the yard, making it stink. From the fields, a swineherd sounded his horn to gather his pigs.

"This," Don Quixote told himself, "is a great castle with a moat and towers. Hark! A magnificent trumpet blast is announcing my arrival. Sir," he asked the innkeeper, "are you governor of this noble castle?"

"He's crazy," thought the innkeeper. "And he's a strange man, with his odd, long face. But I'd better not upset him... Er, the governor?" he said. "Yes I am."

"Then take my horse to your stable, and let me rest here tonight after something to eat. But first, get me out of my suit."

The innkeeper unstrapped the buckles and dropped the suit by a water trough, but he couldn't take off the cardboard visor without untying the ribbons.

"Don't touch my helmet!" ordered Don Quixote, afraid it would all fall apart.

"That makes things difficult..." hesitated the innkeeper. "If you want to eat, you'll have to hold the visor open so I can drop food in your mouth. And I'll have to pour in your drink."

As Don Quixote munched his supper in this unusual manner, a muleteer led his mule to the water trough, tripped over Quixote's shield, and hurled it aside.

"Help me, sweet Dulcinea, in this first moment of peril!" whispered Don Quixote. Jumping up, he clonked the muleteer on the head. "You dare to lay one finger on my shield!" he shouted. "You'll pay for it with your life!"

The man fell down, stunned. A second man rushed to help, but Don Quixote hit him too. With two bodies lying senseless in the yard, all the people staying in the inn raced outside and began throwing stones at Don Quixote.

"Vile cowards!" yelled Don Quixote. "Base-born rabble. Come nearer, I'll stand up to you. You'll pay for your insolence."

He sounded so fierce that they stopped. The wounded men were taken away, leaving Don Quixote bruised but triumphant. "Now I have proved my bravery, will you perform the deed of knighthood?" Don Quixote asked the astonished innkeeper.

"I'd better get on with it before there are any more calamities," he thought and, taking Don Quixote's sword, he touched each shoulder, proclaiming: "I name you Knight of the Long Face. May God make you a fortunate knight and give you luck in your battles."

Eager to see the back of him, he added, "I'm not going to charge you for supper, so you can leave first thing in the morning."

"Charge me?" exclaimed Don Quixote. "Money isn't mentioned in any of the adventure books I've read."

"Ah," said the innkeeper, trying hard to avoid another outburst. "Most knights have squires who keep supplies in their saddlebags — money, clean shirts, ointment to cure wounds and so on."

Don Quixote rubbed himself where the stones had hurt him. "What a good idea."

As he jogged away on Rocinante's scrawny back, his brain sizzled with decision. "Now I'm the Knight of the Long Face, I must get myself a squire."

Chapter 3
Treacherous windmills

"Don't go away again," begged his niece when he got home. "You're ill. Believing you're a knight – it's ridiculous!"

"Let me get back to my books," urged Don Quixote. "They're not ridiculous."

But it was too late. While he'd been away, his housekeeper had made a huge bonfire and burned them all. The priest and the barber had walled up the library door, so he couldn't even find his empty shelves. Furiously, he felt over the place where the door used to be. At last, worn out with raving, he went to bed.

The following morning, he crept out secretly to sell some land to pay for his next adventure.

On the way back, he met Sancho Panza, a farmer who lived nearby.

"You can't miss the opportunity of being my squire," said Don Quixote in his most persuasive voice. "Just think what glittering prizes you might win with me: money, treasure, land... If I conquer an island, which could easily happen, I'll make you governor."

"Oh," gulped Sancho Panza. He grinned.

"We'll set off this very night!" decided Don Quixote. "Don't forget saddle bags and don't tell a soul."

That evening, Sancho Panza, with the bags and a leather bottle strapped to his donkey, rode proudly next to Don Quixote. Crossing a huge plain, they espied thirty or forty windmills in the distance.

"Look!" shouted Don Quixote. "Over there – thirty or more terrible giants whom I will fight and kill."

"Giants? Where?" asked Sancho Panza.

"Over there," pointed Don Quixote, "with the long arms. These giants have arms almost six miles long."

"Those aren't giants," Sancho retorted. "They're windmills. What you think are arms are in fact their sails. When the wind turns them, they turn millstones."

"You don't know anything about adventures," replied Don Quixote. "They're giants, and if you're frightened, you can hide and say your prayers while I fight them." He sank his spurs into Rocinante and charged them at top speed, calling as he galloped, "Help me, sweet Dulcinea..."

"Flee not, you evil creatures," he cried. "Only one brave knight attacks you!"

A gust of wind arose and the sails began to move. Don Quixote shrieked, "But you have more arms than any giant should have, and I will make you pay for that."

He thrust his lance into a sail, but the wind turned the sail so fast, it smashed the lance to smithereens, dragging the horse and his rider with it. Don Quixote went rolling over the plain with yelps of pain.

Sancho Panza prodded his donkey and rushed to help. "Didn't I tell you to be careful? Didn't I say they were windmills?"

"You don't understand," Don Quixote replied, struggling back onto his horse. "An evil enchanter has just turned all these giants into windmills to deprive me of my glorious victory."

"And now you're riding all lopsided," Sancho observed.

"I know." Don Quixote, wincing, tried to sit straighter. "But do I moan? Never! Knights are not allowed to grumble, no matter how severe their wounds."

"I'm glad I'm only a squire, not a knight," said
Sancho, swigging a drink from his leather bottle.
"I'm going to moan like anything if I get hurt."

Don Quixote wasn't listening. He tore off a dead
branch from an oak tree. "This will be my new
lance," he cried, fixing on the iron head from the
broken one. "We'll spend the night under these trees
and see what happens tomorrow."

Chapter 4
Deceitful sheep

In the morning, after breakfast, Don Quixote noticed a huge, dense cloud of dust approaching them along the road. He almost purred with delight. "See that, Sancho? My great deeds today will be written in the book of fame for future generations to admire. That dust is coming from a vast army of countless different nations marching towards us."

"In that case there must be two armies," said Sancho. "Because opposite it, back there behind us, is another dust cloud, just like it."

Turning around, Don Quixote saw that Sancho was right. "These two armies," he proclaimed, "will clash in the middle of this vast plain. The army in front is led by the great Emperor Alifanfarón; the army coming up behind belongs to his enemy, Pentapolin, King of the Garamentes."

"Why do these two lords hate each other so much?" asked Sancho.

"Because..." replied Don Quixote, thinking rapidly. He could picture the scenario so clearly, he was convinced it was real. "This Alifanfarón loves King Pentapolin's daughter, and the King won't let them marry because Alifanfarón is a pagan, and Pentapolin's a Christian."

As the dust clouds loomed ever larger, Don Quixote, more excited by the minute, even began naming the knights in each army, pointing out their flags. "Listen, Sancho. Can't you hear the horses, the bugles, the beating of the drums?"

"All I hear," said Sancho, "is lots of sheep bleating." He was right.

Two flocks of sheep were coming closer, flanked by shepherds.

"You're too scared to see properly," scoffed Don Quixote. "Stand aside while I support one of these armies."

He whipped up old Rocinante into a gallop, waved his lance and sped across the plain like a thunderbolt.

"Come back," yelled Sancho. "I swear by my sword it's sheep you're charging."

"Follow me, knights of the Emperor!" cried Don Quixote, ignoring Sancho as he galloped straight into the army of sheep, spearing them with fury. "I am the Knight of the Long Face."

"Stop!" shrieked the shepherds. When they found Don Quixote was unstoppable, they drew out their slings and pelted him with stones until he fell down, squealing with agony. Quickly, they rounded up their flocks and raced away.

"Are you badly wounded?" panted Sancho, running as fast as he could to where Don Quixote lay.

"I think they've knocked all my teeth out." Don Quixote staggered stiffly to his feet. "But knights never complain. I'd rather lose teeth than my sword arm."

"Didn't I tell you they were sheep?"

"It just shows," replied Don Quixote, "my old enemy, the enchanter, is up to his tricks again. Envious of the glory that was just a breath away from being mine, he turned the armies into a flock of sheep. I was on the knife-edge of victory. Never mind, Sancho. Another adventure awaits us on another day."

Chapter 5
The sour fruit of freedom

The very next day, as Don Quixote and Sancho Panza trotted down the road, they passed twelve men walking in a line, strung by the neck like beads on a great iron chain, with shackles on their hands. Accompanying them were two men on horseback and another two on foot.

"Look – a chain gang of prisoners on their forced

march to the sea. They're off to be galley slaves, roped to the oars to row the King's ships," remarked Sancho.

"WHAT?" thundered Don Quixote. "You mean they're being forced, against their will, to march to slavery? How can the King allow it?"

"It's not like that," Sancho tried to explain. "They're criminals. They've done very bad things. This is their punishment."

"Whatever the rights and wrongs, this is a situation that calls for ME. The relief of the wretched. The redressing of outrage."

"Leave them alone," advised Sancho.

"I'll have a word with them first," said Quixote. "What did you do?" he asked one of the chained-up men.

"I was a horse thief," replied the prisoner.

"And you?" he turned to another.

"I stole some wine."

"What about you?" he asked a third.

"Be quick," snarled a guard, threatening the prisoner with his stick. "This one's a dangerous villain who's committed more terrible crimes than the rest of this gang."

"You weren't given that stick to ill-treat us," this prisoner retorted boldly. "My name is Pasamonte. I've been in worse places than this and escaped... I'm no coward. Let's just get on with what must be done and make no fuss about it."

"I've heard enough!" shouted Don Quixote, moved by these brave words. "Guards, these poor men haven't done any harm to you. Let them go."

The guards split their sides laughing. "This man's a lunatic," they cackled. "Come on. Joke over."

"It's not a joke," cried Don Quixote, hitting one of the guards. Taken by surprise, the guard fell to the ground.

"Stop!" screamed the remaining guards, surrounding Don Quixote menacingly.

Sancho drew his sword. Though he was frightened, he slashed away so fiercely that the guards fled, terrified for their lives.

Quickly the prisoners seized their opportunity and smashed the chain that imprisoned them.

"I've given you and your friends freedom, Pasamonte," Don Quixote exulted. "In return, do one thing for me. Go at once to my Lady, Dulcinea del Toboso, and tell her every detail of this adventure, so she knows how valiant I've been."

"Don't be so daft," Pasamonte replied. "Of course I won't. I'm not hanging around for you or the Holy Brotherhood."

"The Holy Who?" asked Sancho.

"The police, you ignorant oaf. They'll be looking for us now and they're vicious. I'd better disguise myself... I know: I'll steal your clothes!"

Pasamonte snatched the coat Don Quixote had on, stripped off Sancho's hat and stockings and cleared off as fast as he could. The other prisoners had already disappeared.

"Ungrateful wretches!" yelled Don Quixote, shaking his fist to the empty air.

"Oh dear," shivered Sancho, his bare knees knocking together. "That horrible Holy Brotherhood will be after us too, for setting them free. We'd better go."

Don Quixote swung himself onto Rocinante's back. "How could they treat us so badly, when we did so much for them?" he asked, bewildered.

For once Sancho had no answer.

Chapter 6
Mad with passion

Don Quixote and Sancho forged their way through forest ravines up to the lonely mountains to hide from the police.

"At least those rapscallion prisoners didn't pinch our saddle bags with all our food," said Sancho, peering inside them. "Salami and wine. Yum. Let's sit down and have lunch." Then he added, quaking, "I hope the bears don't get us."

"This is the perfect place for an adventure, Greedy-guts, not a picnic," said Don Quixote. "All my books feature knights wandering in wild mountains."

Daydreaming happily, Don Quixote noticed a bag disintegrating under a pile of leaves. "Quick, Sancho!" he called. "What's this?"

"Ooh!" squealed Sancho, ripping the rotten leather open. "Four fine shirts. Lots of gold coins. And a dirty old notebook. Someone's written a silly poem. Listen." He read aloud:

Where gods are cruel and love is blind
Misery has pierced my mind...
Let me die, for I am sure
Without Lucinda, there's no cure.

"Aha," said Don Quixote. "It's obvious what this is all about. A knight has been rejected by his love and has come here to die in his loneliness. I have to admit, though, knights are more noted for their bravery than the elegance of their verse. Why don't you take the money, Sancho, and keep it for yourself? I don't want it."

"At last! An adventure that pays cash!" exclaimed Sancho, stuffing the coins into his own saddle bags. "Hey, what's over there?" He pointed in the distance where a wild man, half naked, with a thick beard and a pony tail, leaped over rocks.

"Our poet, I expect," Don Quixote said. "Let's follow him."

"N-No," murmured Sancho, "because then I might have to give this lovely money back."

"Well, yes," Don Quixote replied. "Or you'll be guilty of stealing."

"But he looks crazy," Sancho moaned. "I don't suppose he wants it."

"You should ask him. Do your duty, and hold your head up high."

They soon caught up with the wild man who greeted them politely, and then cried, "If you people have anything to eat, for God's sake, let me have it."

"Poor, ravenous Ragged Knight," Don Quixote whispered. "Sir, my whole desire is to help you," he said courteously. "All that is mine, consider yours. Eat your fill and tell me, who are you and what brought you here to this wilderness?"

After eating, the Ragged Knight stretched himself out on the grass. "This is my story. Don't interrupt, please. I'd like to get it over quickly since to dwell on my misfortunes is to add to them."

"I promise," said Don Quixote, sitting beside him. "And so does Sancho."

"I am Cardenio, a nobleman from Andalusia. I have loved Lucinda from childhood, and she loved me. I asked, and was granted, her father's permission to marry her. Then I received a letter from Duke Ricardo, the most powerful noble in Spain, demanding my services as companion to his son, Fernando.

I left my home and Lucinda to earn gold for her. Fernando and I became friends. He is young, handsome, fun. I told him about Lucinda, her beauty, wit and intelligence and he..."

Cardenio broke down, weeping, before forcing himself to continue. "He betrayed our friendship. He sought out Lucinda and, as his family is richer and grander than mine, he easily persuaded her father that he, not I, should be her husband."

"Shocking!" exclaimed Don Quixote.

"He married her. He stole her from me, though he was already engaged to be married to Dorotea." With these words, Cardenio drummed his feet and waved his arms in circles. "Agh!" he screamed and flattened Don Quixote with his fists.

"Uh-oh, he's going crazy. Better get out of here," Sancho advised, jumping on his donkey. Don Quixote staggered into his stirrups, and they rode away.

Cardenio, howling with misery, ran off and disappeared between the shadowy mountain peaks.

"It makes you think, Sancho," Don Quixote said. "Fernando's treachery... I don't want anyone stealing my Lady Dulcinea from me. Pen and paper, please."

Sancho got them out of his saddle bag and watched as Don Quixote scribbled:

Noble Lady,
Sweetest Dulcinea del Toboso
If your beautiful self scorns
me, my life is not worth living.
Say you will be mine, or I will
end it — to satisfy your cruelty
and my desire.
Your Own,
Knight of the Long Face

"A very good letter," said Sancho, buckling up his saddle bag and smacking it with satisfaction, stuffed as it was with the Ragged Knight's coins.

Sancho had no intention of finding Dulcinea. Instead he planned to ride straight to the nearest inn and order a large hot dinner. He was tired of snacking on cold food. "What will you eat while I'm gone?" he asked Don Quixote, feeling a twinge of guilt.

"Fruit from the trees," Quixote replied. "I will be half naked and miserable, like Cardenio. I've learned a lot about knightly conduct from him. Take Rocinante. Tie your donkey to his harness; you'll get there faster."

So saying, Don Quixote ripped his shirt in two
and began to wander, carving poems onto the bark
of trees.

HE SOUGHT ADVENTURES
AS HE PINED
FOR HIS QUEEN,
WHOSE EYES ARE BLIND.

Chapter 7
Costumes and confusion

When Sancho reached an inn, he was surprised to see the priest and the barber from his own village.

"Where's Don Quixote?" they demanded. "You've got his horse."

Sancho explained the terrible effect of Cardenio's story on Don Quixote. "Here's his letter to Dulcinea." He searched in the saddle bags and turned his pockets inside out.

"Oh no! I've lost it."

"She hasn't a clue who he is anyway," said the
priest, "so that doesn't matter. What does matter is
getting him home."

"How...?" mused the barber.

"Suppose..." said the priest thoughtfully, "I dress
up as a girl and pretend to be a damsel in distress.
You," he pointed to the barber, "pretend to be my
squire. You must ask Quixote to save me from a
wicked knight, by taking me to a secret destination,
without asking questions. Then we can whisk him
back home."

"Brilliant!" said the barber.

The innkeeper's wife lent them a dress, and the
barber created a beard from a cow's tail. The priest

looked as pretty as a picture.

"Oh dear," he said, gazing in the glass. "I look unsuitable for a man in my profession. Let's swap."

The barber agreed. Now he looked as pretty as a picture, and the priest wore the cow's tail beard.

Sancho guided them towards the spot where he'd left Don Quixote. They stopped by a river, stumbling over Cardenio, who was amazed that the priest and barber knew his story from Sancho.

"Listen... can you hear singing?" asked the priest.

A young boy in farmer's clothes was paddling in the river shallows, singing a sad song in a sweet, high voice.

"Look at his hands!" whispered the barber.

"I see what you mean," the priest replied softly. "Small and white as alabaster. That's a girl in disguise."

"Almost as lovely as Lucinda," blurted Cardenio. The boy certainly displayed a face of extraordinary beauty.

"My Lady... for surely you are a lady, do you need help?" offered the priest.

The beauty instantly burst into tears. "No one can help me. I am Dorotea, from Andalusia. I was going to be married, but Fernando, my beloved, jilted me for a girl from a noble family, unlike poor me."

"Fernando!" Cardenio gulped.

"I raced to make him marry me. I love him still. But I was too late. I discovered that his bride, Lucinda, had fainted during the wedding, while taking her vows. Just before she fell unconscious, she declared she loved Cardenio. She only agreed to wed Fernando because her parents had forced her and she swore to kill herself with a dagger.

The priest dissolved the marriage and Fernando rode off in a rage. As for Cardenio, he had already disappeared. I ran away, too miserable to start a new life, and wandered into these mountains."

While she was speaking, a smile formed on Cardenio's face that spread into the widest grin.

"I am Cardenio," he declared. "I won't rest until I see you married to Fernando, while I..." He flung his arms up to the sky with joy. "I will marry my lovely Lucinda. My madness is cured."

"Excellent," said the priest. "Now we must look after Don Quixote."

"The famous, crazy knight?" Dorotea was so happy, knowing she would be reunited with Fernando, that she wanted to make all the world happy too. Hearing Don Quixote's predicament, she turned to the barber. "Lend me your pretty dress. I have an idea..."

Chapter 8

Demons
in the ox cart

Don Quixote sat under a tree, half naked,
his clothes dangling from a branch above.

Dorotea threw herself at his feet. "Are you
the Knight of the Long Face?" she asked. "I
am Princess Mircomicona. A giant has stolen
my land and threatens to eat my father. Can
you help me?"

"A beautiful damsel in distress?"
responded Quixote warmly.
"I'll do everything
I can for you."

"Will you promise not to get involved in any other adventure until you've sorted mine out?" pleaded Dorotea.

"I swear," answered Don Quixote. "Sancho, help me with my suit."

Hidden behind another tree, the barber laughed so much that his beard fell off. Quickly, he stuck it back. Cardenio was disguised in the priest's hooded cloak, while the priest — strutting uncloaked in his doublet and hose — was unrecognizable. They followed Don Quixote, Sancho and Dorotea across the plain to the inn.

"Don't get upset with the man in the suit," the priest told the innkeeper. "'He's crazy but harmless."

"I heard the Holy Brotherhood want him."

"Please don't tell them," begged the priest. "We're taking him home."

"He can sleep in the barn loft where I keep my wine. Out of harm's way," the innkeeper replied kindly.

But at midnight, Sancho screamed, waking the

entire inn. "Come quickly! My master's fighting...
There's blood everywhere..."

"EVIL CREATURE!" Don Quixote yelled,
brandishing his sword.

"He's slashed my wineskins," roared the
innkeeper in fury, looking at the floor awash with
a lake of red bubbles. "My best vintage, ruined!"

"I've killed Princess Mircomicona's giant," Don
Quixote triumphed. "It was a fierce battle, and
I won."

"You've wounded wineskins," scolded the innkeeper. "As you'll realize when you get my bill."

"This room is too sodden with blood to sleep in," yawned Don Quixote wearily. "I'll go downstairs."

In the hall two ghostly figures with white faces and dark cloaks seized him, dragged him to the courtyard, and threw him in a wooden cage which they hoisted onto an ox cart. Sancho found himself tossed beside his master. There they sat, bruised and dazed, clutching the bars of their prison.

"Knight of the Long Face," chorused scary voices. "An enchanter sends you and your squire into the unknown. He asks you to promise to go on no more adventures for a year. Do you swear?"

"Y...Yes," quavered Don Quixote.

"Then we'll leave you."

"I never read of transport like this in my books," Don Quixote complained to Sancho. "Knights are usually whisked off on magic carpets. But I'll do as that enchanter says."

The demons grinned. "It's worked," they chortled, jiggling the ox cart reins. The priest and the barber took off their cloaks and scrubbed the paste from their faces. They were taking Don Quixote home to La Mancha.

Chapter 9
Farewell good knight

Don Quixote woke up to find himself back in his own bed.

His niece and housekeeper, overcome with relief, constantly brought him tempting trays of food and drink.

"Thank goodness you're safe. We've been so worried," they chorused.

Don Quixote felt curiously weak, now that he was not expending all his energy on adventures. He stayed in bed, remembering how he had wandered in search of danger with Rocinante and Sancho Panza.

Sancho came to visit him. "Someone's written a book about you," he announced. "Look... You're famous, just as you wanted."

"Let me see," Don Quixote flicked the pages. It was a big book, with illustrations of the knight on Rocinante, dwarfing Sancho and his donkey, tilting at windmills, charging over the wide Spanish plains.

"I'm not sure about it," Sancho said. "It makes you out to be a figure of fun. It's easy to ridicule, harder to be fair, especially when the truth is not obvious. The Don Quixote I know is brave, wise and kind – righter of wrongs, a protector... This Don Quixote, the one in print, is a mockery."

"I don't feel very well," yawned Don Quixote, sinking back into his pillow. Just before he fell asleep he muttered, "I'd like to see a doctor, a lawyer and the priest. I think I'm going to die."

"He's suffering from melancholy," said the doctor, when he came. He felt Don Quixote's pulse. It was very low.

His friends gathered around. "We must help him," they insisted.

But there was nothing they could do. Don Quixote was fast asleep, and they feared he would never wake up.

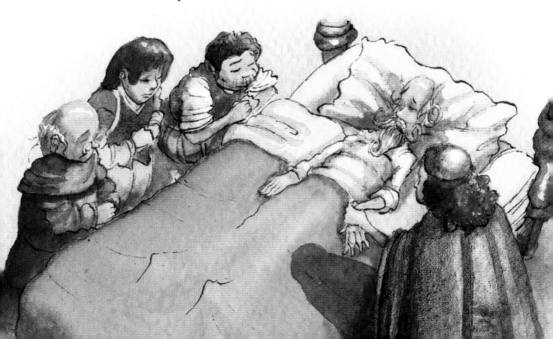

At last he did.

"I must make my will," he announced with a smidgen of his old energy. "I am no longer Don Quixote de la Mancha, but rather Alonso Quixada. I was crazy; now I am sane. So near death, I will not joke about names or noble deeds."

Sancho was unashamedly in floods of tears. "Get up... Let's go on adventures again and have fun. Don't die of grief — it isn't worth it. A disappointed knight today is a conqueror tomorrow."

Don Quixote hardly listened. "I leave you a sum of money, Sancho, so that you can lead a good and useful life. My housekeeper shall likewise have money... and to my niece, I leave all my household goods, with the proviso that if she marries a man who has a library of adventure books, she forfeits all that is mine."

With these words, Don Quixote closed his eyes and breathed his last.

That was the end of the Knight of the Long Face. His friends had an epitaph carved on his tombstone.

Don Quixote

*He never cared what
people thought –
A clown to pompous eyes.
He lived his life a gallant fool
And finally died wise.*

The Three Musketeers

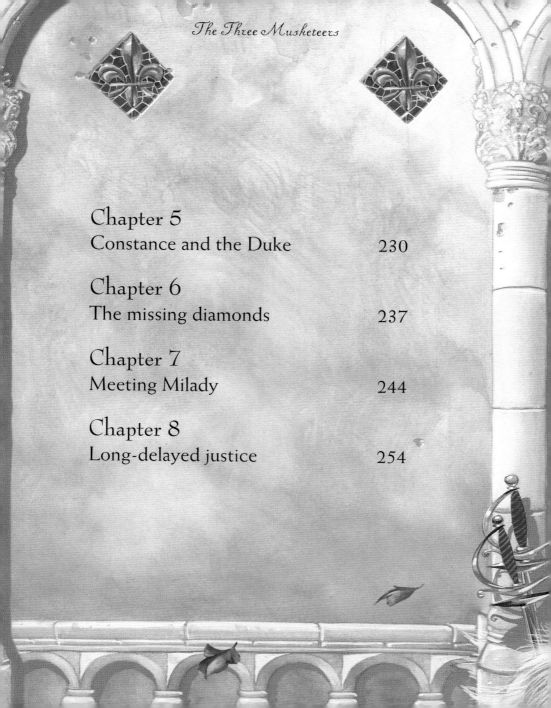

Chapter 1
The ugliest horse in the world

When d'Artagnan left home, his father gave him three things: 15 gold coins, a letter of introduction to the captain of the musketeers in Paris, and a remarkably ugly yellow horse.

Everywhere d'Artagnan went, people noticed his horse. Then they noticed the sword hanging from his belt and decided to keep their thoughts to themselves.

Just outside Paris, d'Artagnan came to a little pub called the Jolly Miller and met a man who couldn't help laughing at the ridiculous animal.

"Have you seen that creature?" the man guffawed to his friends. "It's as yellow as a buttercup!"

D'Artagnan was young and proud and he couldn't let an insult go unchallenged. "Mock my horse," he snarled, "and you mock me. I challenge you to a duel, sir!"

The stranger laughed and, for the first time, d'Artagnan noticed a ragged scar which ran the length of his cheek.

"A duel?" he scoffed. "Surely you know that the King has banned them."

D'Artagnan wouldn't be put off. He drew his sword and lunged for the man. The stranger quickly pulled out his own sword, but before the fight could begin, d'Artagnan felt something heavy hit the back of his head. Desperate to stop the fight, the barman had knocked him out.

When d'Artagnan woke, his head throbbed painfully. He looked around and saw the scarred man talking to a woman inside a horse-drawn carriage.

"You must go back to England, Milady de Winter," the scarred man told the woman. "Inform the Cardinal as soon as the Duke leaves London."

The man spurred his horse and, before d'Artagnan could stop him, he'd galloped into the distance. "Blast him!" d'Artagnan cried. "Now I shall never avenge his insult!"

His voice died out as he got a close look at Milady's face. She had golden hair, huge blue eyes and rose-red lips, and d'Artagnan thought she was the most beautiful woman he'd ever seen.

"Milady," he said. For one moment her eyes met his – then she gave a quiet command and the carriage sped off into the distance. D'Artagnan stared after it, wondering if he would ever see her again.

Chapter 2
The Three Musketeers

The following day, d'Artagnan was in Paris, his eyes wide as he rode through the streets. He'd never seen a city so grand, bustling with people and lined with imposing houses built from golden stone.

Soon he was at the house of Mr. de Treville, the captain of the King's musketeers, the most famous soldiers in France. For as long as he could remember, d'Artagnan had wanted nothing more than to serve in that élite force.

"Mr. de Treville might be able to spare you a few minutes," said the servant who answered the door, sniffing disapprovingly as he studied d'Artagnan's shabby clothes.

D'Artagnan swallowed nervously, but he held his head high as he walked into the room. Mr. de Treville was wearing a frown so fierce it could have curdled milk. He ignored d'Artagnan completely and instead bellowed, "Athos! Porthos! Aramis! Come in and see me at once!"

Two men rushed into the room. Porthos was tall with a long black moustache and an even longer nose, which he gazed down at everyone around him. Aramis was smaller and thinner and his face was as innocent as a child's. Neither man paid any attention to d'Artagnan.

"I hear you've been duelling with the Cardinal's guards," de Treville snapped. "And worse than that – you lost! What do you have to say for yourselves?"

"It's true we were defeated," Aramis said indignantly, "but that's because we were outnumbered and taken by surprise."

"Athos was very badly injured," Porthos explained, as a third musketeer entered.

Athos was older than his two friends and would have been strikingly handsome if he hadn't been so pale. "Nonsense!" he declared. "It was just a scratch." But his lips were thin with pain.

"I suppose you did your best," de Treville said reluctantly. "Just don't get caught like that again." The three musketeers bowed and left. "And what do you want?" de Treville asked d'Artagnan, seeming to notice him for the first time.

"I want to join the musketeers," d'Artagnan declared, though inside he was filled with uncertainty. How could he ever match up to the men he'd just seen?

De Treville appeared to feel the same. "An inexperienced boy like you join the most famous regiment in France?" he scoffed. "No, if you want to become a musketeer, you must first prove yourself worthy of our uniform." He looked as if he doubted d'Artagnan could do it.

Just then, d'Artagnan glimpsed a man out of de Treville's window. It was the scarred stranger who had laughed at his horse. Without even calling goodbye, d'Artagnan ran out after the man.

D'Artagnan was moving so fast, and his attention was fixed so firmly on the stranger, that he didn't see Athos until he'd bumped right into him. "Watch it, you fool!" shouted Athos.

"Who are you calling a fool?" d'Artagnan said indignantly. "You're the one in the way."

"I'm not a man to take an insult lying down."
Athos spoke haughtily, though his hand was clutched
to his side in pain. "I demand that you meet me by
the deserted monastery for a duel at noon tomorrow."

All d'Artagnan could think of was the man with
the scar, who was in danger of disappearing into the
crowd. "Fine," he said. "Tomorrow I'll teach you
some manners." Then he ran off, eyes still fixed on
the man he was pursuing rather than the people
around him.

This time it was Porthos who stood in his way. D'Artagnan found himself tangled in the other man's magnificent cloak – revealing the threadbare clothes Porthos was wearing underneath.

"You young whippersnapper!" Porthos bellowed. "You've made me look ridiculous. I demand satisfaction. We'll cross swords at the deserted monastery at one tomorrow."

D'Artagnan didn't even answer. He simply nodded and carried on running after the stranger. It was no use; the other man had made good his escape.

"Bother!" d'Artagnan exclaimed. "I've lost my quarry and offended two strangers. I really must try to be more civil in future."

So when he passed Aramis, d'Artagnan decided to be as friendly as possible. "Sir, it appears you've dropped something," he said, picking up a handkerchief from the ground beside Aramis.

Aramis was furious. The handkerchief had been given to him by a female admirer, and he'd been hoping to keep it secret. "Interfere in my business, will you!" he snapped at d'Artagnan. "I'll soon teach you better – when I defeat you in a duel at two o'clock tomorrow. Be waiting at the deserted monastery."

Shoulders slumped, d'Artagnan slunk back to his lodgings. He'd come to Paris to make his fortune, and instead he'd made three deadly new enemies.

Chapter 3
Three duels before tea

"Are you alone?" Athos asked d'Artagnan, when the two men met the following day. "It hardly seems right to kill a man who doesn't have a friend in the world."

"I'm the one who should feel guilty," said d'Artagnan, "for fighting a duel with an injured man."

It was true that Athos didn't look well. His face was as white as the clouds scudding across the sky, and his arm was clutched to his wounded side.

"I tell you what," d'Artagnan offered. "Why don't I let you have some of my mother's special ointment? You can put it on your wounds and when you're feeling better we'll meet again for our duel."

Athos was impressed with his gallantry. "That's very noble, sir, but even injured as I am, you won't find me an easy match."

D'Artagnan bowed and drew his sword. Before the duel could begin, two more men arrived: Porthos and Aramis.

"You're early!" d'Artagnan exclaimed. "It's an hour before I'm due to fight Porthos and another two hours until I'm meeting Aramis."

"Hold on!" Athos said. "You've both arranged duels with this man?"

"So it would appear," Porthos said. "He must be a very hot-tempered fellow."

"Well, when I'm through with him, there won't be

much left for you two to fight,"
said Athos.

He lunged towards d'Artagnan
and their swords met with a
metallic clang.

"Halt!" a voice shouted. "Duels are against the law!" It was the Cardinal's guards. Soldiers of the Cardinal, the King's right-hand man, they despised the musketeers and were delighted to have found an excuse to arrest one.

"You're not taking Athos without a fight," Porthos declared, as he and Aramis drew their own swords.

D'Artagnan looked between the groups: the Cardinal's guards, who had probably just saved his life, and the musketeers who had been planning to take it.

"If there's going to be a fight," he said, "there's only one side I can take – the King's musketeers!" He flourished his sword as he went to stand beside Athos, Porthos and Aramis.

There were five guards and four of them, but d'Artagnan was fighting beside three of the finest swordsmen in the land.

Aramis struck, faster than lightning, and thrust his sword into his opponent's heart. Another guard cried out as Porthos plunged his blade through his leg.

Athos fought hard as well, but his wound slowed him down. D'Artagnan leaped forward, putting his own body between a guard's sword and Athos's chest. In a second he'd disarmed the guard and rescued Athos.

The fight was over. D'Artagnan and the three musketeers were on their feet, but all five guards lay on the ground.

Athos turned to smile at d'Artagnan. "I think I shall have to call off our duel. It doesn't seem right to kill a man who's just saved my life."

Aramis and Porthos nodded their agreement.

"It was a privilege to fight by your side," d'Artagnan said, bowing. "From now on, we should always stick together. One for all, and all for one, that's what I say."

The three musketeers liked this new motto very much. "All for one," they chorused, "and one for all!"

Chapter 4
The landlord's sister

O ver the next few weeks, d'Artagnan tried to find out more about his new friends. Aramis, he discovered, dreamed of being a priest rather than a fighter. Porthos cared about nothing but beautiful clothes and beautiful women. He spent his free time chasing after rich widows.

Athos, however, remained an enigma. He never laughed and seldom smiled. Sometimes, d'Artagnan thought he detected a deep sadness in his companion, but whenever he asked Athos about it, the other man would shrug and change the subject.

D'Artagnan was still pondering the secret of his friend's past when he heard a knock on his door. It was his landlord, a short man with a high opinion of himself.

"Oh, Mr. d'Artagnan!" he said, walking into the house without being invited. "Something awful has happened and you're the only one I can turn to. My sister Constance has been kidnapped!"

"Why would anyone want to kidnap your sister?" d'Artagnan asked.

"She works for the Queen," his landlord explained. "And the Queen has powerful enemies. They hope to prise the Queen's secrets from my poor sister."

"That is terrible," d'Artagnan agreed. "And as a

musketeer — or at least a musketeer in training — I'm bound to protect the royal family. Do you know who took her?"

"I don't know his name but I'll never forget his face," said his landlord. "He has a scar running the length of his cheek."

"That man!" d'Artagnan exclaimed.

"I think he's one of the Cardinal's agents," his landlord went on. "It's well-known that the Cardinal hates the Queen. I'm sure he's behind this."

D'Artagnan prowled the streets of Paris searching for Constance, but she seemed to have vanished completely. After a fourth day of fruitless searching, he returned miserably to his house. Before he could enter, he noticed a light shining next door. It was his landlord's house – but he knew his landlord was out searching for his sister.

D'Artagnan drew his sword from its scabbard, then flung the door open.

Inside, he was amazed to see a young woman, no older than himself. Her hair was blonde, her face was soft and he thought that she was very pretty.

"What are you doing here?" he asked uncertainly, lowering his sword.

"What are you doing here?" she retorted. "This is my brother's house."

D'Artagnan realized in amazement that he'd found Constance.

Chapter 5
Constance and the Duke

Constance explained that she'd escaped her kidnappers by knotting bedsheets into a rope and letting herself down from her prison window.

"So you didn't need my help after all!" d'Artagnan exclaimed, impressed with her bravery. "But why did they kidnap you?"

"That is someone else's secret," said Constance. "I can't reveal it to you. And now I'm afraid I must go."

D'Artagnan didn't want to let this intriguing young woman leave. "The people you escaped may still be chasing you," he said. "Let me guard you."

Constance refused and left the house before d'Artagnan could argue.

Still, he decided that he had better make sure she was safe. He crept after her along the quiet, late night streets of Paris, sticking to the shadows so she wouldn't know he was following.

Eventually she came to one of the many bridges crossing the river. She had just stepped onto it, when a man approached her from behind and grabbed her shoulder.

"Let go of her!" d'Artagnan roared, leaping out and tearing the man's hand away from Constance.

"D'Artagnan!" she said angrily. "What are you doing here? I told you not to follow me."

"I thought you might need protection and I was right," he said, glaring at the man.

Constance sighed. "This man isn't my enemy," she explained. "He's the Duke of Buckingham. I was sent here to meet him by the Queen."

"But why would she want you to meet an English nobleman?" d'Artagnan asked.

"Because the Queen loves me and I love her," said the Duke.

Like all good Frenchmen, d'Artagnan hated the English, but this man seemed an honest, likeable person.

"I came to France in secret to see the Queen," the Duke continued, "but Constance tells me that the Cardinal's agents are hunting for me. They'll kill me if they find me."

"Then I shall guard you both," declared d'Artagnan. "No one will dare to attack you with me by your side."

D'Artagnan was as good as his word, and got them safely into the palace.

As soon as he saw the Queen, the Duke took her in his arms. "Oh, I've missed you!" he said.

Although the Queen didn't love the King, having been forced to marry him when she was very young, she knew she had to keep her wedding vows. "Please return to England," she begged the Duke. "We can never be together... but take this as a token of my love." And she handed the Duke a beautiful rosewood box. Inside were twelve diamonds on a ribbon, a present to her from the King.

What the Queen didn't realize was that someone else was watching.

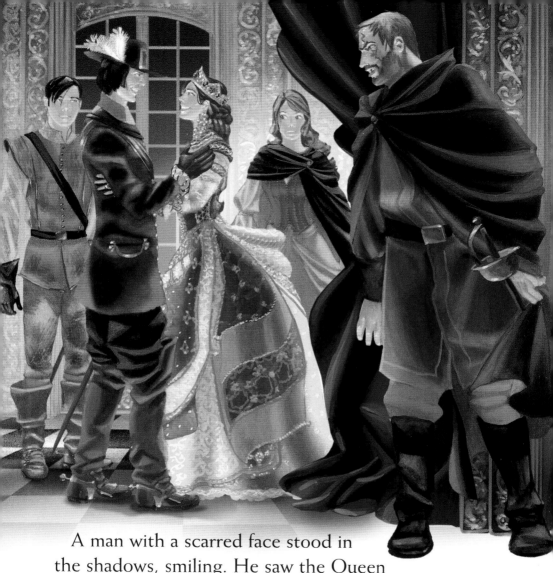

A man with a scarred face stood in
the shadows, smiling. He saw the Queen
hand over the diamonds, then ran to tell the Cardinal.

The next day, the Cardinal suggested the King hold a ball for the Queen. "Tell her to wear the diamonds."

The Queen turned pale when she heard. "Somehow he must have found out that I've given them away."

"Don't despair, your Majesty," said Constance. "I'll ask d'Artagnan to go to England and fetch them."

She found him at duelling practice. When d'Artagnan saw Constance again, he thought she looked even prettier than he remembered. He agreed to her plan at once. He might not survive the trip, but it would be worth the risk if it meant Constance fell in love with him.

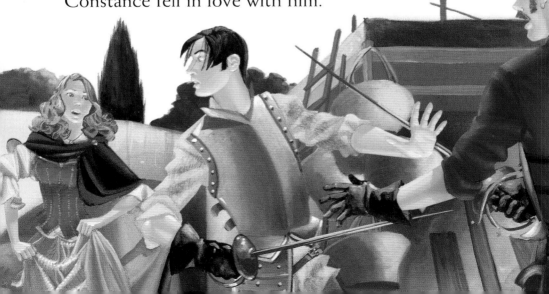

Chapter 6
The missing diamonds

D'Artagnan told his three friends about the mission and they insisted on coming along. "Remember," Athos told him. "It's all for one and one for all."

Unluckily for them, the Cardinal had discovered the plan, and he was determined to do everything in his power to stop d'Artagnan from reaching England.

Porthos was the first to fall foul of the Cardinal's plotting. In a small inn on the outskirts of Paris, an agent of the Cardinal provoked him into a fight. Porthos won the duel, but he didn't escape unscathed. Reluctantly, d'Artagnan left his friend behind to recover from his wounds.

D'Artagnan, Athos and Aramis rode on into the night, but the danger was far from over. The Cardinal had organized an ambush on the road that led to the coast.

D'Artagnan and Athos galloped through as arrows rained around them, but Aramis was thrown from his horse. D'Artagnan wanted to stay and help him, but he'd made a promise to the Queen. With a heavy heart, he spurred his horse on.

When they reached the coast, they stopped at an inn overnight. But the innkeeper too was the Cardinal's agent, and, while d'Artagnan slept, he imprisoned Athos in his cellar.

D'Artagnan searched the inn, but he couldn't find Athos anywhere and there was no more time to waste. Sighing, he paid his passage and boarded the first ship bound for England – completely alone as he sailed to a dangerous foreign land.

The crossing was stormy and the English were unwelcoming, but d'Artagnan didn't let that put him off. He was determined to save the Queen.

D'Artagnan finally found the Duke hunting in the countryside with the English King. "Your Grace," he called, as he leaped off his horse. "I bring a message from the Queen of France. She needs you to return her diamonds. Without them, she'll be disgraced."

The Duke looked sick.

"Oh no," he said. "I've kept them in the box but when I last looked, two were missing."

"You've lost them?" yelled d'Artagnan.

"No." The Duke shook his head. "I believe they were stolen by Milady de Winter, an agent of the Cardinal's who lives in London."

As he described Milady, d'Artagnan realized that it was the very same woman he'd seen talking to the man with the scar, in the carriage all those weeks ago.

"Well, I can't return to France without the diamonds," d'Artagnan told the Duke. "Constance will never forgive me."

"Don't panic," said the Duke firmly. "I'll hire the best goldsmith in the land to cut and polish two new ones. No one will be able to tell the difference."

Three days later, the Duke had twelve diamonds once again. "Here," he said, giving them to d'Artagnan. "I only hope it's not too late."

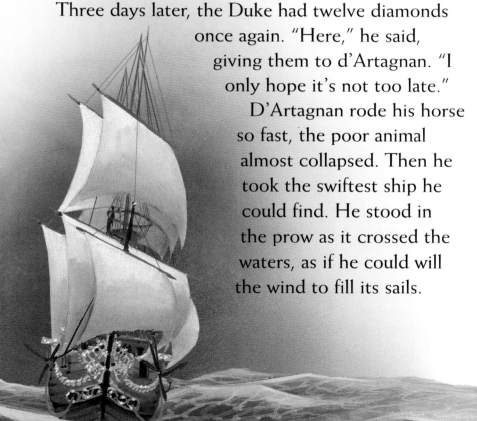

D'Artagnan rode his horse so fast, the poor animal almost collapsed. Then he took the swiftest ship he could find. He stood in the prow as it crossed the waters, as if he could will the wind to fill its sails.

Finally, he raced back into Paris just as the ball was about to begin.

The Queen was in despair. As soon as she saw d'Artagnan with the diamonds, her face broke into a huge smile. "You did it!" she cried.

"I would do anything to serve you, your Majesty," d'Artagnan said, but he was looking at Constance as he said it.

Chapter 7
Meeting Milady

A few days later, d'Artagnan received a note from Constance. "Come and meet me at the summerhouse outside the city," it read. She wanted to see him! D'Artagnan was delighted.

He rode to the summerhouse at once. But when he arrived, he found it ransacked. Chairs were broken, books were scattered all over the floor — and there was no sign of Constance.

Desperately, he asked people living nearby if they had seen what happened.

"It was a man with a scar," a woman told him. "We saw him carrying Constance away, kicking and screaming."

"The Cardinal's agent," d'Artagnan thought bitterly. "He's taken Constance because we helped the Queen."

D'Artagnan tore back to the city to beg his friends for help.

"This is what happens when you fall in love," said Athos. "Women were put on earth to bring misery into our lives."

Porthos laughed. "Nonsense! Besides, what would you know about it? I've never even seen you speak to a woman."

"I was married once," Athos said quietly. "She was the love of my life. But after our wedding I saw a flower-shaped scar on her shoulder, the brand of a common criminal. She'd been caught stealing from the Church. I threw her out of my house. I've not let myself love another woman since."

Still, he agreed to help d'Artagnan hunt for
Constance. The four men searched all of Paris and
outside the city too. They spoke to her brother
and they asked the Queen, but no one knew where
Constance was.

Walking home in despair, d'Artagnan spotted a
head of golden hair in the crowd. She turned – and
he recognized Milady de Winter.

"She works for the Cardinal too," d'Artagnan muttered to himself. "She must know where Constance is."

The next day, he presented himself at Milady's house, dressed in his finest clothes. "I've come to pay court to the most beautiful woman in France," he declared.

He wasn't alone. D'Artagnan found out
that many men were pursuing Milady, though
she seemed to like just one, a sour-faced
nobleman called the Count of Wardes. She was
polite to d'Artagnan, but he sensed distrust
lurking behind her wide smile.

"She sounds dangerous," Athos had said.
"You should stay away from her."

But d'Artagnan was sure she was his only hope of finding Constance. Day after day, he returned to pay her compliments – until he had a piece of luck. He intercepted a letter Milady had written to the Count of Wardes, asking him to meet her in secret later that night.

Milady never guessed that the man behind the curtain was d'Artagnan and not the Count.

"Thank goodness you've come," she said, sounding sweeter than she ever had when she spoke to d'Artagnan. "I've been having the most miserable week!"

"Why is that?" asked d'Artagnan, speaking softly to disguise his voice.

"That dreadful d'Artagnan has been visiting me every day," she said. "How I loathe that man."

"You do?" D'Artagnan was puzzled.

"He ruined all my plans," Milady replied. "Thanks to him, I nearly lost my position with the Cardinal. He's an interfering, arrogant, strutting young fool!"

This was too much for d'Artagnan, who leaped from behind the curtain. "Not such a fool that I can't trick you!"

Milady backed away in horror.

"Now tell me where Constance is," d'Artagnan demanded.

"Your little damsel in distress? The Cardinal asked me to send her somewhere you'll never find," she sneered. She pulled a knife from beneath her bodice and lunged for him.

D'Artagnan grabbed her arm to stop her. The knife clattered to the floor and her dress ripped beneath his hand. Underneath it, her shoulder was marked with a brand in the shape of a flower.

Milady pulled herself from his grasp and scrambled from the room.

D'Artagnan was too startled to move. Milady was a common criminal — and she was branded in the same place as Athos's long-lost wife.

Chapter 8
Long-delayed justice

Athos was shocked to discover that the woman who had helped to kidnap Constance might be the same criminal he had once married.

He helped d'Artagnan break into Milady's house to search for clues. Athos paused, a wistful expression on his face, when he found an antique ring in a cabinet. "This was a family heirloom," he said. "I gave it to her on our wedding day."

At last, they found what they were looking for — a letter arranging for Constance to be held in a convent.

"Don't worry d'Artagnan," Athos reassured him. "We'll get Porthos and Aramis and rescue her."

The convent lay many miles outside Paris, and even on the fastest horses the journey took hours. D'Artagnan and his three friends rode through the night, desperate to rescue Constance.

But when the convent finally loomed in front of them, they saw Milady's carriage outside, its open door creaking in the wind.

Inside, Milady was speaking to Constance. "I'm a friend of d'Artagnan's. He sent me to rescue you."

There was something about the other woman that Constance didn't trust. "Why didn't d'Artagnan come himself?" she asked.

Milady smiled sweetly. "Here, drink a glass of wine with me and I'll explain."

Constance took a glass from Milady. She hadn't noticed her sprinkle powder into it. She watched as Milady drank, then sipped the wine herself.

As soon as Constance's glass was empty, Milady smiled again, a vicious smile this time. "I think I hear d'Artagnan," she said, as the gate to the convent clanked open. "A shame you won't get to speak to him."

For a moment, Constance was confused. Then she felt a terrible heaviness spreading through her body and fell to the floor. "Have... you... poisoned me?" she choked.

Seconds later, d'Artagnan and the three musketeers rushed in. D'Artagnan fell to his knees beside Constance.

She looked at him, her face twisted with pain. "I love you," she whispered, as her eyes closed.

"I should have killed you when I had the chance," Athos told Milady bitterly. "You'll pay for this."

The four men took Milady outside and held a trial. "The punishment should be death," d'Artagnan declared and she was executed. Justice had been served, but it wouldn't bring Constance back.

As soon as d'Artagnan set foot in Paris, he was summoned before the Cardinal. He assumed he was to be punished for what he had done to Milady.

Instead, the Cardinal said, "You're a brave, honest man, d'Artagnan. I'm very sorry that Constance was killed. Those were never my orders. I can't bring her back, but I can give you something else that you value." He handed d'Artagnan a piece of paper, stamped with his official seal. It was a commission to serve as a lieutenant in the King's musketeers.

D'Artagnan had finally achieved his dream. Alongside his three friends, he would serve his King proudly – the youngest of the Four Musketeers.

THE 39 STEPS

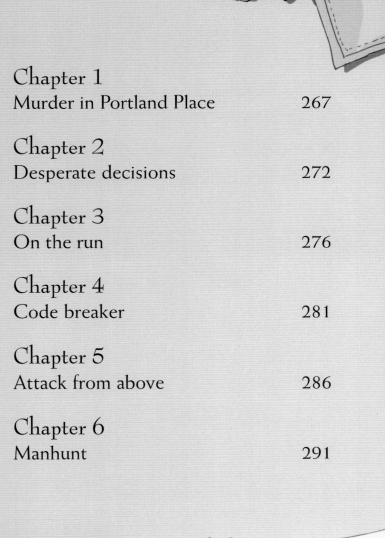

Chapter 1
Murder in Portland Place

On that muggy June night in 1914, I must admit that I was feeling rather fed up with London.

Having spent most of my life as a mining engineer in the wilds of Rhodesia, my return to England had been tediously dull by comparison.

Yet as I approached my rented house that evening, little could I have imagined the breathtaking adventures that lay ahead of me.

I had just turned my key in the lock, when a slim, bearded man appeared from nowhere and bundled me indoors.

"What the devil...?" I began.

"Pardon the intrusion, Mr. Hannay," panted the stranger as I tried to regain my composure.

He dashed across to the window and peered down cautiously at the street below.

"How do you know my name?" I asked.

"Oh, I know a fair deal about you," he replied, drawing the curtains. "Chiefly that you're a man to be trusted."

Despite my better judgement, I was intrigued by the young fellow.

"My name is Scudder, Franklin P. Scudder," he announced. "And I need your help, sir."

"I'll listen to you," I replied, switching on the light. "But that's all I'll promise."

Scudder took a seat with his back to the window. "Mr. Hannay, here in London, on June fifteenth, an attempt will be made to assassinate a man named Karolides."

I'd read about this Karolides in the papers. He was the Greek Premier and just about the only one who could prevent a war in Europe, by all accounts.

"If I can lie low 'til that date," continued Scudder, "I might prevent a catastrophe."

I was becoming even more interested. "But who would want Karolides dead?" I asked.

"A group of foreign agents known as the Black Stone. They're on my tail, and they'll stop at nothing to get me." The young man's eyes darted towards the window. "The head of that illustrious organization is particularly interested in making my acquaintance."

The look on his face spoke volumes. This gang leader was obviously a force to be reckoned with.

"He's a master of disguise, Mr. Hannay," he went on, raising his right hand, "but if ever you encounter a man missing the top joint of his fourth finger, then be on your guard."

The whole tale seemed far-fetched. Yet if this fellow was spinning me a yarn, he was a darn good actor.

I thought for a moment. I'd wanted excitement. Well here it was, right on my own doorstep.

"Very well, I'll trust you," I said at last. "I believe you're straight – but if not, I should warn you that I'm a handy man with a gun."

He clasped my hand. "Thank you, Mr. Hannay," he said warmly. "You won't know I'm here."

The next four days passed rapidly and Scudder was as good as his word. He spent most of his time closeted in my study, scribbling away in a small black notebook.

Then, on the fifth day, I returned home in the early hours of the morning.

I switched on the hall light and opened the drawing room door. The scene illuminated before me sent a shudder of horror down my spine.

There on the floor lay the body of Franklin P. Scudder – pierced through the heart by a knife.

Chapter 2
Desperate decisions

Having assured myself that poor Scudder's killers were no longer in residence, I considered my position. The devils must be aware that Scudder would have taken me into his confidence. How long before they tried to dispose of me in a similar fashion?

And here I was with a dead body in my home. If I went to the police, they were hardly likely to believe my story about assassination attempts and foreign agents. What I needed was evidence... Of course, the notebook!

My earlier inspection of the house had alerted me to the fact that Scudder's killers had been looking for something. Drawers, cupboards, even the clothes in my wardrobe had all been rifled. Now I knew the reason why.

After a long, fruitless search of my own, I slumped down despondently into an armchair and took out my pipe. Plunging my hand into the tobacco jar at my elbow, I felt something curious. I could hardly believe it. There in my grasp was the very thing I'd been hunting for.

I flipped through the pages of the little black book, hoping to find some answers, but the whole thing was written in code.

While I consider myself as being pretty sharp when it comes to cyphers, after an hour or so racking my brain I was no further forward. I realized this puzzle would take time to crack.

My only hope was to lie low somewhere remote until I had the evidence to make the Government take Scudder's warning seriously. The Scottish Borders seemed the best bet.

I edged slowly to the window and looked down at the street. It was empty, save for a tall figure standing on the corner opposite. Was he a member of the Black Stone? Had he seen me return? I couldn't take any chances.

Quickly, I changed out of my evening clothes and into a sturdy tweed suit. Glancing at the railway timetable, I stuffed Scudder's notebook and a few essentials into my pockets. The fire escape outside the kitchen led me down to a deserted alleyway at the rear of the building. So far, so good.

I checked my watch and broke into a sprint. The express train to Scotland would be leaving Saint Pancras in ten minutes.

Chapter 3
On the run

When I reached the station there was no time to buy a ticket. I barged past the platform officials, and jumped into the last carriage of the Scottish express with seconds to spare.

As the train rattled north, I pulled Scudder's notebook from my pocket. I was pretty certain that all I needed was a keyword to unlock the code. But as the hours passed, everything I tried failed to make any sense.

Eventually I dozed off, and I only just woke in time to change at Dumfries. A slow Galloway train took me through a land of little wooded glens to a great wide moorland, gleaming with lochs and fringed by rolling hills.

As the compartment filled with locals, I felt as if every one of them was eyeing me with suspicion.

Then I caught sight of something that only heightened my anxiety. The man next to me had a copy of the mid-day edition of *The Scotsman*. There on the front page screamed a headline that made my blood run cold.

PORTLAND PLACE MURDER

Killer flees north?

POLICE investigating the brutal murder of an as yet unnamed man in a London apartment block have reason to believe that the killer may have travelled north. Border offi-

The police would have wasted no time contacting the ports and stations with my description. Those officials at Saint Pancras must have remembered me.

I suddenly became aware of two men opposite who were engrossed in the same newspaper. They must have read the report. Was there a description of me? Could it be that I had already been recognized?

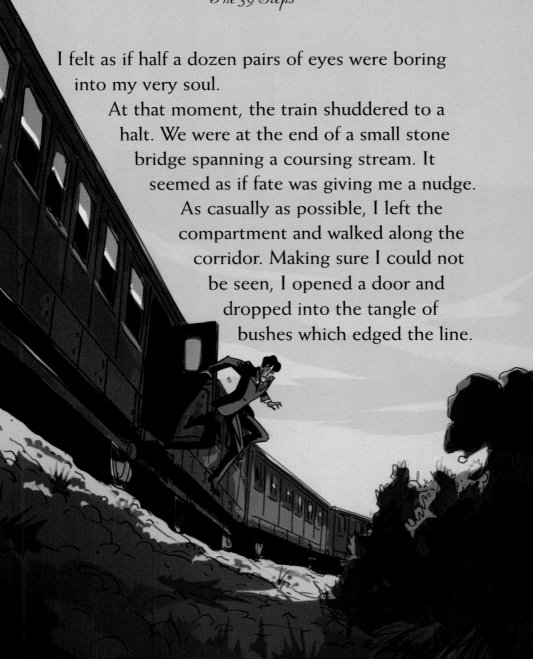

I felt as if half a dozen pairs of eyes were boring
into my very soul.

At that moment, the train shuddered to a
halt. We were at the end of a small stone
bridge spanning a coursing stream. It
seemed as if fate was giving me a nudge.
As casually as possible, I left the
compartment and walked along the
corridor. Making sure I could not
be seen, I opened a door and
dropped into the tangle of
bushes which edged the line.

I scrambled through the thicket, reached the edge of the stream and soon found cover in the bushes a hundred yards away.

From my hiding place, I could see the reason for the train's sudden halt. A stray sheep had wandered onto the line ahead. Luckily, the guard who had already alighted to remove this obstruction had clearly been too busy to notice me. He herded the beast clear of the track, and within five minutes the train was on its way.

I only hoped that no one on board had witnessed my dramatic departure.

Chapter 4
Code breaker

There was no time to dwell on what might have been a hasty decision. I broke cover and continued my journey across country.

At about six that evening, I came to a rough stretch of road where the welcoming lights of a solitary inn sparkled in the twilight.

A good night's rest did wonders for my optimism, and the next morning I felt ready to pit myself against Scudder's code once more.

For the best part of three hours I wrestled with the contents of the little black book, until finally it dawned on me. What if 'Black Stone' were the keywords?

I was proved right. Soon I had the bones of Scudder's discoveries in front of me.

They didn't make for pleasant reading. Scudder believed that immediately after Karolides' death, top secret details of British military security were to be stolen from a diplomat who was due to convey them to our allies in France. The thieves would hand this information to the German Government. Being thus assured of victory, Germany would declare war on Britain.

Despite my efforts, the precise meaning of some of Scudder's notes remained obscure, such as a dozen odd references to *thirty-nine steps*. Their last mention was followed by the phrase *I counted them – 10:17 p.m., high tide.* I could only hope they weren't too important.

Whatever the significance of these cryptic passages, the basic knowledge I had in my possession was explosive enough to be taken seriously. Somehow I had to find a way to alert the authorities to the situation.

At that moment, I heard the sound of a motor car approaching. I went to the window and saw a touring car pull up a few hundred yards away. Two men got out and walked towards the inn. One was squat and muscular. The other resembled the man I'd seen outside Portland Place.

I crept along the corridor to the hallway. From there I could hear what was said in the lobby without being seen.

Momentarily I heard the front door open and the two men enter. They were greeted by the innkeeper to whom they proceeded to give an all too accurate description of myself.

I didn't wait to hear any more. I scuttled back to my room, opened the window and scrambled outside. Keeping low, I ran past the inn and along the road to the men's car. I started it and, sending up a shower of gravel, raced away from the inn as fast as I possibly could.

Chapter 5
Attack from above

Any doubts I might have had as to whether the Black Stone were on to me vanished in an instant.

I drove the forty horse-power tourer across the moor roads for all she was worth. I could only hope that having deprived my enemies of their vehicle, I could put a fair distance between them and myself.

After half an hour or so I dared to hope that I'd shaken off my pursuers. Then, glancing behind me, I saw something that set my pulse racing.

Far in the distance, a monoplane flew low over the hilltops. For a moment this sinister craft circled as if getting its bearings. Then, with a burst of speed, it headed straight in my direction. I could hear its engine buzzing louder and louder above me, like some tormented insect.

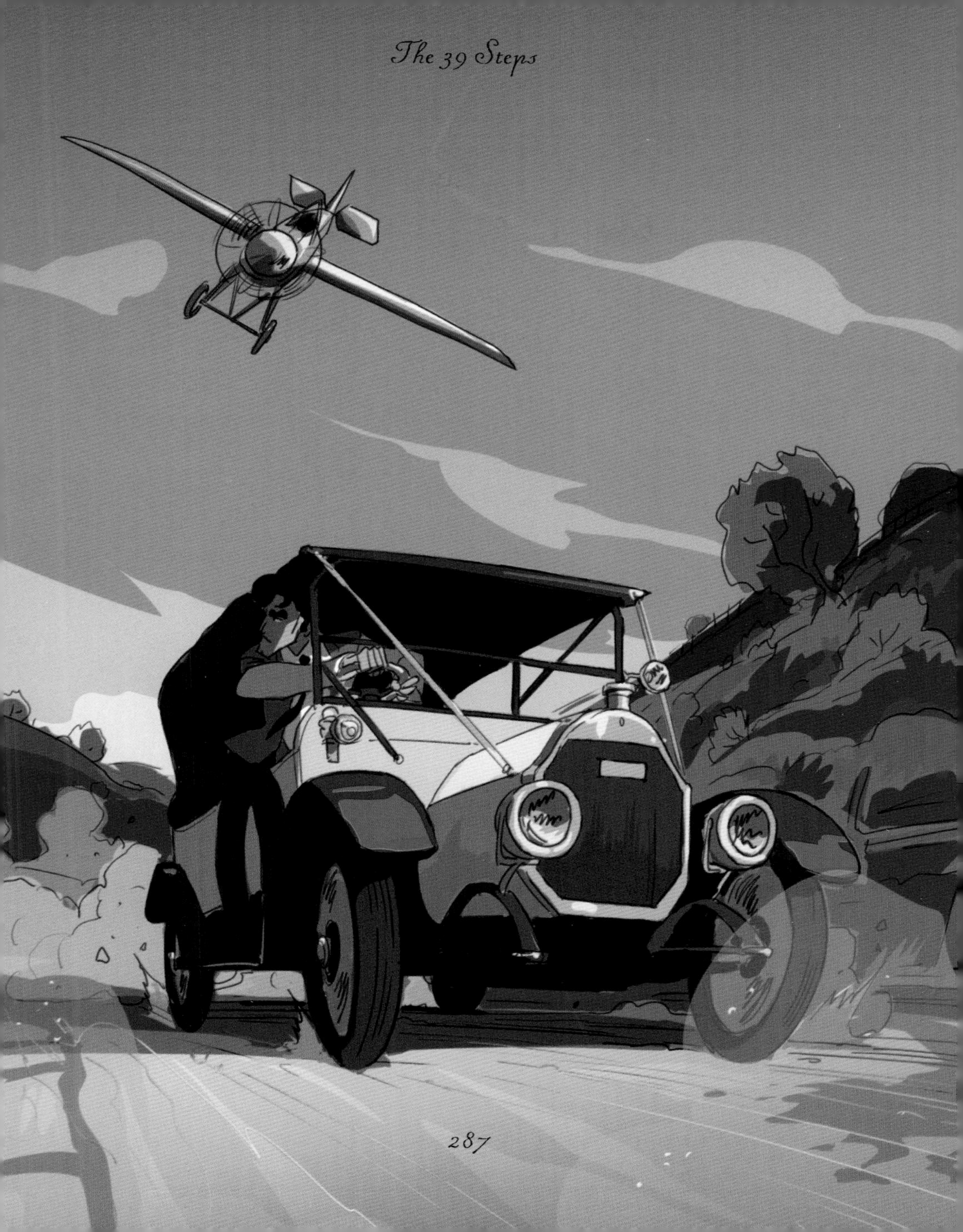

If my stalkers had taken to the air, then my chances of evading them were dramatically reduced. On the bare moor I was at their mercy. My only chance was to get to the leafy cover of the valley.

I hurtled down the hillside like lightning. The bumpy roads were better designed for sheep than motor cars, and it felt as if my bones might rattle clean through my skin.

I had no choice but to go on, looking back when I dared, only to see the plane getting closer and closer.

Soon I was on a road between hedges. The noise of the aircraft seemed fainter behind me now, and I let my concentration slip for a second.

At that moment, I caught sight of the nose of another vehicle emerging at ninety degrees from a driveway ahead of me.

The road was too narrow to steer around the other car, so I took drastic action. I crashed into the hedge on the other side of the road.

As hawthorn
branches
scratched at
my face, I sensed
the ground beneath
the car give way. To my
horror, I realized that
the hedge bordered a sheer
drop to a river, some thirty feet
or more below.

I felt the car buck and pitch. Then
something hit me full on the head.
I had a vague sense of an almighty
smash, then nothing.

Chapter 6
Manhunt

"Steady there, old chap," came a warm, friendly voice.

As I blinked back into consciousness, the figure of a tall young man in tweeds formed before me.

He pressed a glass into my hand and I gulped down the contents gratefully.

I found myself lying on a sofa in what seemed to be some grand manor house.

"I must apologize for pulling out in front of you like that," he said. "Bad show."

"Er, no, it was my fault," I rambled. "You're not hurt, Mr...?"

"Bullivant, Sir Harry Bullivant. No, not a scratch, dear boy. Which is more than can be said for your motor car, I'm afraid."

"It seems I have you to thank for my lucky escape," I said, rubbing my sore head.

"Thank that hawthorn branch, old man, not me," he said with a chuckle. "Hooked you like a jolly old salmon and left you dangling. I just reeled you in, so to speak."

Over dinner, I engaged in the most pleasant conversation with my new friend, without giving away too much about myself.

As we finished dinner he told me that politics ran in his family, as his uncle was the Permanent Secretary at the Foreign Office.

This news forced me to reconsider my secrecy. Here was someone with a link to the authorities. I had to risk taking Harry into my confidence. Today was the thirteenth. If Scudder was right, the attempt on Karolides' life would be made the day after tomorrow.

"Listen here, old man," I said. "I've something of a confession to make." I proceeded to tell him the whole story. He listened patiently, and when I'd finished he sat thoughtfully for a minute.

"I may be a bit of a chump as a politician, but I can size a chap up," he said at last. "You're no murderer, and I believe you're speaking the truth. Now, what can I do to help?"

We arranged a plan. He would telephone his uncle, Sir Walter, telling him to expect me at his country home in Wiltshire where I would deliver Scudder's information in person.

Harry offered me the use of his car, but I decided that I would be less conspicuous journeying on foot, cross-country.

After a night's rest, a change of clothes and a hearty breakfast, I took my leave of my new ally and headed south towards the nearest railway station at Moffat.

But I had only been walking for half an hour when I became aware that I was not the only soul in the tangle of glens that morning.

Just over a ridge, in the far distance, I could make out the heads of a string of men — it was the police, assisted by shepherds or gamekeepers by the looks of them.

They hallooed at the sight of me, and I could tell by their sudden excitement that Richard Hannay was their quarry, rather than some unfortunate fowl.

I ran for what felt like several miles.

Breathlessly, I breasted the top of a ridge and found myself in the grounds of a whitewashed house. My pursuers had left me no room to retreat. I had no choice. I would have to take my chances inside the building. I sprinted across the lawn and walked through a pair of French windows. Inside, seated at a desk, was an elderly, bald headed gentleman. He didn't move, but simply stared at me with raised eyebrows.

"You seem in a hurry, my friend," he said calmly. Unable to catch my breath, I nodded towards the window at the line of approaching men.

"A fugitive from justice, eh?" he said. "Well, we can discuss it at length later. In the meantime, I've no desire to have clumsy rural policemen disturbing my peace." With that, he ushered me down a hallway and into a tiny cupboard-like room. "You will be safe enough here," he said, before closing the door behind him with a click.

Hardly able to believe my luck at the gentleman's kindness, I crouched in the darkness. As the minutes passed, I could make out neither the sound of my protector nor my pursuers. Then suddenly the door opened and the old man reappeared.

"They've gone," he assured me. But my relief was cut short by his very next words. "This is a lucky morning for you, Mr. Richard Hannay."

Before I had time to take this in, the old man raised a revolver to my head.

A glance at the man's right hand confirmed what I should have realized the moment I set foot in the house.

I was face to face with the leader of the Black Stone.

Chapter 7

The lair of the Black Stone

"Let us not waste time with formalities," said my captor, extending that tell-tale hand. "The notebook if you please."

"What notebook?" I replied flatly.

"Come now, Mr. Hannay," he said with a cruel smile, "We've come too far to play games." As if to emphasize this point, he inched his revolver closer to my head.

"Who is this Hannay, guv'nor?" I said, trying to sound more confident than I felt. "Ned Ainslie's my name, and so help me I wish I'd never gone and pinched that cursed motor car."

For a second I saw the villain's eyes flicker with doubt. He gestured with the gun for me to leave the room. Keeping me covered all the while, he frog-marched me back into the study. Then he rang a small bell and two men entered. I recognized them at once as the sinister characters from the inn.

"Well, Franz?" asked the bald man.

"That's him," said the taller of the new arrivals.

"Relieve Mr. Hannay of the contents of his pockets, Karl," ordered his boss.

The squat fellow grabbed me roughly and disgorged what little I had onto the table. To my surprise, I realized that the notebook was missing.

The bald man's voice took on an impatient tone. "Where is it?" he rasped threateningly.

"I already told you, guv'nor..." I began.

"Lock him up!" barked the chief to his lackeys. "We'll see if a spell without food and water loosens his tongue."

I found myself being manhandled across a courtyard and into a damp, pitch black storeroom attached to the main house. As my jailers turned the key in the lock, I tried to make out anything that might aid my escape.

After groping around, I found a cupboard and managed to force it open. On the shelf in front of me were a box of matches and several electric lamps. Taking one, I examined the rest of the contents.

There was a carton of detonators, cord for fuses, and a dozen little bricks. Crumbling one in my hand, I recognized it at once as lentonite. I hadn't been a mining engineer for nothing. With just one of these bricks I could blow the house to smithereens.

I picked up a detonator and attached it to a couple of feet of fuse. Then I put the detonator in a quarter of a lentonite brick and buried it under a sack near the door.

Crouching as far away as possible, I lit the fuse and waited. I only hoped that I would survive the next few moments intact.

Suddenly a wave of heat surged from the floor. Then the wall opposite flashed a golden yellow and dissolved with a thunderous roar that hammered my brain into a pulp.

At first, I felt myself being choked by thick yellow fumes. But then fresh air wafted in from a ragged rent in the wall.

Clambering over the debris, I stepped through the hole and out into the yard.

I could hear confused cries coming from the house. Running blindly through the smoke, I managed to find my way to the fringe of trees that surrounded the building.

Then I kept running until I had put a good two miles between myself and the villains' lair.

Chapter 8

Assassination

After an hour or so tramping across country, I finally reached the town of Moffat.

As I approached the station, my heart was lifted by the sight of young Harry Bullivant.

"Thank heavens," he cried. "I thought I might have missed you. I say, you do look a fright."

I swiftly related my encounter with the Black Stone.

He responded by putting his hand into his pocket and producing a familiar black tome.

"Scudder's notebook!" I gasped.

"I had you down as a chump for leaving it in your old jacket pocket, dear boy. But I reckon that little blunder saved your skin."

I thanked my new friend profusely and after he had lent me the rail fare to Wiltshire, I bade him a sad farewell.

Harry's uncle turned out to be a square-jawed fellow who welcomed me into his home as if I were family. I showed him Scudder's notebook and told him of the young man's warning regarding Karolides. It emerged that Scudder had been known to the British Secret Service and was highly regarded.

Sir Walter was persuaded some dark business was imminent, but to my surprise he dismissed Scudder's theory about an assassination as fanciful. "In any case," he added, "Karolides is too well guarded."

After a bath, a shave, and a change of clothes, I explained everything that had occurred to me, from the death of Scudder to my encounter with the Black Stone.

"Being chased right into the very house they'd rented was a stroke of bad luck," said Sir Walter.

"I still don't know how the local police got onto me," I said.

"After Harry telephoned, I did a bit of research on your adventures," said Sir Walter. "It seems the innkeeper told the police about the car you stole.

They found the wreckage and then picked up your trail nearby."

"I suppose I'm still a wanted man," I said with a sigh.

"Oh, I've sorted all that out with Scotland Yard, dear boy," said Sir Walter, with a reassuring smile.

We spent the next few hours poring over Scudder's notes, interrupted only when Sir Walter had to leave the room to take a telephone call.

When the distinguished man returned, his face was ashen.

"It seems I owe our late friend Scudder an apology," he said sadly. "Karolides has been shot dead."

Chapter 9
The imposter

I glanced at my watch. It was a few minutes after midnight. Karolides had been murdered on the fifteenth just as Scudder had predicted.

"War is inevitable now," said Sir Walter. "We shall have to bring Royer's visit forward."

"Royer?"

"The French diplomat. He'll be taking the details of Britain's military security back to France."

"Can't you cancel it?" I asked.

"No, we must carry on as planned," replied Sir Walter. "It's vital to the safety of Britain and her allies in the times that lie ahead."

Early next morning, we drove to Sir Walter's house in London. It was here that the meeting with Royer was to take place. The event was some hours away, but I was determined to stay and see things through.

That evening, I watched nervously from the
balcony overlooking the hall as Royer and a stream
of well-known officials arrived at the house and
walked past into the meeting room.

When they adjourned, I saw the First Sea Lord
emerge. At least that was my first thought. I had
seen that familiar face in newspapers and magazines
a hundred times – the trim beard, the firm fighting
mouth and the blunt square nose. Yet, at that
moment, as he glanced up and caught my gaze,
I spotted a look of recognition in his keen blue eyes,
even though we had never met.

As he left, I rushed down the staircase and picked up the telephone. A few seconds later I was connected with the Sea Lord's residence.

"Is his Lordship at home?" I asked.

"His Lordship retired to bed an hour ago," said the servant. "He is unwell tonight."

It seemed my part in this business was not yet ended. I marched into the meeting room and was met by the questioning faces of the assembled officials.

"Gentlemen," I announced, "the man who just left this room was an imposter."

Chapter 10

A race against time

"Impossible!" snorted Travers, the official from the Admiralty.

"Don't you see the cleverness of it?" I said. "You were too interested in other things to question whether or not the First Sea Lord had been invited. It was natural for him to be here, and that put you off your guard."

"The young man is right," said Royer. "His psychology is good. Our enemies have not been foolish."

"But the fiend heard everything," said Travers. "The security plans, not only of this country, but also those of France."

"Then we're done for," I said.

"No, my friend," said Royer. "I know something of the habits of the spy. He delivers his intelligence in person and receives his reward in person."

I was filled with renewed enthusiasm. "Then if we can intercept the Black Stone before they can leave the country..."

"But we've no way of knowing where they'll leave from," said the War Minister.

Suddenly I had a flash of inspiration.

"The thirty-nine steps!" I cried.

The Minister looked at me as if I had gone mad.

"There was a phrase in Scudder's notebook," I explained, "*Thirty-nine steps — I counted them* — 10:17 p.m., *high tide.*"

"Then we've less than twenty-four hours to find them," said Sir Walter.

"Right, gentlemen," I said purposefully. "We'll need a book of Tide Tables."

Minutes later, we were at the Admiralty, scanning the locations where high tide occurred at 10:17.

At first it looked a hopeless task. That time covered at least fifty places.

We had to narrow it down.

Where would a man in a hurry leave for Germany? Somewhere on the Southeast coast I reasoned. That would provide the quickest crossing to Ostend or Antwerp.

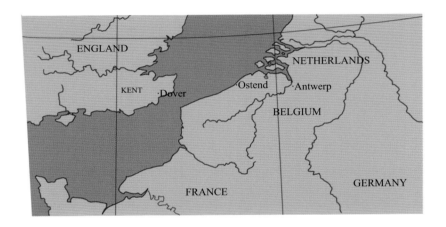

There were no regular night steamers at 10:17, so they must plan to use a private boat that would require a high tide to launch from shore.

Then there were the steps. It didn't sound like a dock somehow. It must be some place where there were several staircases, with one marked out from the others by having thirty-nine steps.

The Inspector of Coastguards was called for, and after a process of elimination we finally came up with a location – the Ruff.

"It's a big chalk headland in Kent," explained the coastguard man. "It has lots of villas on the top, and some of them have staircases down to a private beach."

I looked around the assembled company. "If one of those staircases has thirty-nine steps gentlemen, then we've solved the mystery."

Chapter 11
The thirty-nine steps

By ten o'clock the next morning, I found myself on a clifftop overlooking a row of quaint villas on the Kent coast.

I was joined by Scaife, an Inspector from Scotland Yard with naval experience. He had just returned from a closer study of the staircases of each house.

"There's only one with thirty-nine steps," he
announced.

I almost jumped up and cheered at the news.

"Place called Trafalgar Lodge," he went on.
"Belongs to a respectable old gent called Appleton,
according to the house-agent."

At that moment a yacht came into the bay. She
looked about a hundred and fifty tons and was flying
a white ensign that marked her as one of our own.

"Might be innocent enough," said Scaife. "I'll go
and investigate."

So it was that, thirty minutes later, I watched as a
small fishing boat made its way to within a few feet
of the yacht.

I saw Scaife, looking every inch the local angler, call up to the larger craft. Some uniformed crew members appeared on the deck of the yacht and a brief conversation followed. Then Scaife departed and was back at my side within an hour.

"She's called the Ariadne," he said. "The officers and crew sound as English as you or I, but..."

"What?" I asked anxiously.

Scaife looked thoughtful. "There was nothing English about the captain's close-cropped hair or the cut of his collar and tie."

"That settles it," I declared. "It's time I paid a visit to Trafalgar Lodge."

It was just after nine o'clock that I made my way up the path of that humble little villa. A search warrant from Scaife nestled in my breast pocket, next to my racing heart.

The door was answered by a young maid. I told her my name was Smith, and she ushered me into a large drawing room overlooking the garden, with the sea beyond.

But it wasn't the view that first caught my eye as I entered the room. It was the three figures in evening dress standing before me.

Their features may have been subtly altered by the use of false hair pieces, but I was convinced that these men were the trio who had held me captive in Scotland.

The maid introduced me and withdrew. "Mr. Smith?" said the white-haired old man claiming to be Appleton. "I don't believe I've made your acquaintance."

"Save your breath, sir," I said, with all the courage I could muster. "The game's up. I have here a warrant for the arrest of you three gentlemen."

The old man looked shocked.

"Arrest?" he said. "Good grief, what for?"

"For the murder of Franklin P. Scudder on the 11th of June," I replied.

The tall man raised an eyebrow. "Oh, the Portland Place business. I read about it. But you're quite mistaken," he said nonchalantly, "I, for one, was in a nursing home at the time."

"I was out of the country," said the stocky fellow, adjusting his tie in the mirror.

"And I dined at my club until late that night," added the old man, stroking his white beard.

For a split second I wondered if I'd made the most terrible blunder. Perhaps they were genuine English gentlemen after all?

"So you see you are mistaken, young man," said the old man respectfully. "Now if you don't mind," he added, "we are late for an engagement."

I decided to take a chance. "I'm most terribly sorry, sir," I said, removing my leather glove and extending my right hand. "No hard feelings?"

Instinctively, the old gentleman removed his white evening glove to shake hands. In that instant, he realized his mistake. But it was too late. Both our eyes rested on the fourth finger of his bare right hand. Suddenly, he kicked over a table and produced a revolver from his pocket.

"Schnell, Franz," he cried, "das Boot, das Boot!"
The tall man and his compatriot made a dash for the
door, but ran straight into Scaife's men who were
stationed outside. The old man fired a shot at the
police and Franz managed to struggle free. I lunged
at the old man and tackled him to the ground,
sending his weapon flying from his hand. I dragged
him to his feet, just in time to see Franz descend the
steps to the waiting yacht.

"He is safe," cried the old man. "You cannot follow in time. Der Schwarzestein has triumphed."

"Not for long, my fine friend," I said, as I clinked a pair of handcuffs around my prisoner's wrists. "You see, for the last hour, the Ariadne has been in British hands. Those steps lead straight to the hangman's noose."

As you will know, Sir Walter was proved right. War was declared a few weeks later, and I joined up immediately to fight for King and country.

But I still think I'd done my best service before I even put on my uniform.

ABOUT THE AUTHORS

Alexandre Dumas

1802 - 1870

Alexandre Dumas was born in France in 1802. His father was a General in the army and died when Alexandre was only four. After that, Alexandre grew up virtually in poverty, living with his mother and grandparents in the French countryside.

At 21, Dumas went to Paris to seek his fortune. He had always been a great reader and soon he was writing — plays at first, and then novels. These were printed as serials in magazines and drew him a huge audience. *The Three Musketeers*, published in 1844, was a great success and was followed two years later by *The Count of Monte Cristo*.

Dumas was one of the first authors to write lively, exciting, historical stories and combine them with romance and adventure. As a successful novelist, he earned a fortune, but his lifestyle cost even more. He died in 1870, once again in poverty, and was survived by a son who shared his name. His son also became a famous novelist, so today they are often known as Alexandre Dumas père (father) and Alexandre Dumas fils (son).

Sir Anthony Hope
Hawkins

1863 - 1933

Born in London in 1863, Anthony Hope was the son of a vicar. His father ran a school for sons of the clergy and Hope was his pupil for a while. Then he won a scholarship which took him to public school, where he began his writing career editing the school newspaper. He went on to Oxford University and qualified as a lawyer, though he was always writing in his spare time. He thought up the idea for *The Prisoner of Zenda* while walking around London and it took him just one month to write.

When it was published, the novel was so successful that he decided to give up law to become a full-time writer. It has since been adapted numerous times for film and television. Hope also wrote a sequel, *Rupert of Hentzau*, and several other books set in imaginary countries. In all, he wrote more than 30 books and plays, though *The Prisoner of Zenda* remains the most popular. During the First World War, he wrote pamphlets for the Ministry of Information, which earned him a knighthood.

Anthony Hope died at the age of 70, in 1933.

Miguel de Cervantes Saavedra

1547 - 1616

Miguel de Cervantes Saavedra, born near Madrid in Spain, had a life as full of adventure as his hero. After an unsettled childhood, he joined the army and during a sea battle his left hand was badly maimed. Some years later, he was kidnapped by pirates and spent five years as a slave, despite trying to escape.

Ransomed at last and back in Spain, he started to write, working on novels, plays and poetry, but none of them brought in much money. So he became a clerk and then a tax collector – and was sent to prison twice because of problems in his accounts.

It was in prison that he came up with the idea for *Don Quixote*. At first, he simply intended to poke fun at the knightly tales popular at the time. But his story developed into an epic of over 400,000 words, with comedy, tragedy, romance and adventure. It was an immediate success throughout Europe and is still considered a classic of Western literature today.

This success came late in life. *Don Quixote* was published in two parts: the first in 1605 when he was 58; the second in 1615. He died a year later, aged 69.

John Buchan,
1st Baron Tweedsmuir

1875 - 1940

John Buchan was born in Perth, Scotland and studied at Glasgow University, before embarking on a career which combined writing with politics and diplomacy. After graduating, he worked at the British High Commission in South Africa. While in South Africa, Buchan met William Ironside, a military spy who inspired the character of Richard Hannay.

Back in Scotland, he began working for a publishing company. In 1914, on the eve of the First World War, *The Thirty-Nine Steps* was serialized in a magazine and proved enormously popular. When war broke out, Buchan was invited to write war propaganda and headed to France as a journalist.

After the war, he continued to write and then, in 1927, he was elected as a Scottish Unionist Member of Parliament. In 1935, he was made Governor General of Canada and became the first governor general to travel the whole country. Still, he kept writing. In all, he wrote over 100 books, including many thriller novels, five about the adventures of Richard Hannay. John Buchan died in Canada in 1940.

Cover illustration: Simona Bursi

Edited by Lesley Sims
Designed by Sam Chandler
Digital manipulation by John Russell

With thanks to Sam Noonan

First published in 2011 by Usborne Publishing Ltd, 83-85 Saffron Hill,
London EC1N 8RT, England.
www.usborne.com Copyright © 2011 Usborne Publishing Ltd.
The name Usborne and the devices ♀ ⊕ are Trade Marks of Usborne Publishing Ltd.
First published in America in 2011. UE.